T0146575

GODLY LIVING WITH CONTENTMENT FOR EVERY CHRISTIAN

We are now becoming what we are going to be.

Malcolm J. Borden

THE CHRISTIAN'S BIBLICAL STEWARDSHIP OF LIFE

How Members of the New Testament Church Should Manage
What Really Belongs to God

WESTBOW
P R E S S®
A DIVISION OF THOMAS NELSON
& ZONDERVAN

This book is a work of non-fiction. Unless otherwise noted, the author and the publisher make no explicit guarantees as to the accuracy of the information contained in this book and in some cases, names of people and places have been altered to protect their privacy.

WestBow Press books may be ordered through booksellers or by contacting:

WestBow Press
A Division of Thomas Nelson & Zondervan
1663 Liberty Drive
Bloomington, IN 47403
www.westbowpress.com
1 (866) 928-1240

Because of the dynamic nature of the Internet, any web addresses or links contained in this book may have changed since publication and may no longer be valid. The views expressed in this work are solely those of the author and do not necessarily reflect the views of the publisher, and the publisher hereby disclaims any responsibility for them.

Any people depicted in stock imagery provided by Thinkstock are models, and such images are being used for illustrative purposes only. Certain stock imagery © Thinkstock.

ISBN: 978-1-5127-4121-6 (sc)
ISBN: 978-1-5127-4122-3 (hc)
ISBN: 978-1-5127-4120-9 (e)

Library of Congress Control Number: 2016907452

Print information available on the last page.

WestBow Press rev. date: 05/17/2016

CONTENTS

This work is a *complete* presentation designed to enable all Christians to know and experience *how members of the Body of Christ should manage what really belongs to God* because this is real biblical stewardship.

The Christian life is a *process*, in that our lives are constantly subject to change. God works through our circumstances so that, as we submissively respond to Him and His will, we are and become what He wants us to be for His glory.

This work is based on biblical content, utilizing a literal, grammatical, and historical approach to interpretation. It seeks to provide accurate biblical definitions of key concepts as well as identify biblical precepts and principles concerning the Christian's stewardship of life.

There are seven foundational stewardship principles that define God's ownership of everything as the basis of our stewardship and describe the nature of our responsibility to Him as faithful and contented stewards of the material resources, talents and abilities, and time that He has entrusted to us.

Contentment is an attitude of mind and heart that has learned to be satisfied with God's provision as sufficient, based on trusting God and His promises. Godly Christians who are responsible for material resources beyond the basic essentials must choose how they will exercise trustworthy stewardship of their discretionary wealth.

If we are going to know and do the will of God we must first give ourselves to God. God has granted every believer the privilege and responsibility of giving whether wealthy or poor. It is our trust in God that enables us to give *when* the Spirit directs in keeping with *what* God has already provided.

God uses our vocation to provide our essential material needs as well as to provide discretionary wealth. The manner in which we fulfill our vocational responsibilities should reflect the character of Christ and display the fruit of the Spirit in every dimension of our activity and attitude—including our willingness to genuinely distinguish between needs and wants in order to minister to others.

Our stewardship of talents and abilities should center around our relationship with, our submission to, and our worship of God the Holy Spirit who has taken up residence within us for the purpose of accomplishing the will of God in us, and through us for His glory.

Our responsibility is to manage twenty-four hours of God's time each day with wisdom that enables us to redeem the time in keeping with His will for us.

Everything we need for life and godliness comes through knowledge of Christ attained by faith in His Word. The believer's life can be wholly transformed by a full knowledge of God's Word as the means of experiencing a deep, personal relationship with Him.

EXPRESSION OF THANKS

Because of an overwhelming debt of gratitude, I am compelled to express abundant thanksgiving to God and a special group of His people who, in the course of exercising their obedient life commitment to His will, so meaningfully impacted my thinking and life purpose regarding the strategic value of developing the vital skills essential to understanding, interpreting, applying, and teaching His Word. My commitment to develop the required skills was ignited when I was introduced to dispensational premillennialism and pneumatology (the study of the Person and Work of the Holy Spirit) as a Master of Theology student in Dallas Theological Seminary and has continued for six decades in various venues of teaching and preaching.

Though it would be impossible to individually thank all the people represented in the extended time period and multiple geographic locations, they have played important roles in the writing of this book, though the majority were unaware of their involvement at the time. But it is only appropriate to mention some for whom I am deeply indebted. While at Dallas Seminary, I was privileged to sit under the teaching Dr. John Walvoord, Dr. Dwight Pentecost and numerous other competent professors. But the one who has continued to have the greatest influence in my Biblical and doctrinal development is Dr. Charles Ryrie, perhaps because he has written so much so well, including more than 50 books and editing the Ryrie Study Bible that includes more than 10,000 notes written by him. Some have described him as the "having the gift of simplicity," possessing the rare gift of being able to express complex biblical truth clearly, concisely, and correctly. Finally, because of his work aimed at stabilizing the field of dispensational theology, he has become recognized as an "irenic dispensationalist."

My related doctrinal and theological convictions, commitments and desires have been reinforced and strengthened over the years by working and ministering alongside colleagues, mentors, administrators, scholars, teachers, pastors, etc. in the environs of Bible Colleges (particularly Philadelphia College of Bible), local churches and mission organizations, such as Dr. Clarence Mason, Dr. John Cawood, Dr. Paul Enns, Dr. Richard Williams, Dr. Mal Couch, and Dr. Eugene Williams, just to mention a few.

Finally, the conception of this book, including its purpose, design, the determination of important biblical truth and related doctrines to be included, and the realistic need for such teaching resulted from my preparation for, delivery of, and response to a number of preaching series and Bible teaching courses undertaken nearly twenty years ago. During the next few years additional research, study, writing, and the organization of material followed the decision as time and schedule permitted. But heavy ministry responsibilities and demanding projects, in addition to dealing with the typical family health and aging matters necessitated that the actual writing of the book be put aside at least on a temporary basis. Then some months after caring for my wife during her two year struggle with terminal illness that ended our fifty-eight year marriage, the completing of the book appeared to be returning to the realm of possibility. But God graciously allowed me to encounter a serious medical incident that caused the end of my independent living and transportation, and resulted in my need to relocate in another state with living quarters near my family. In the end, the incident and subsequent changes in life style have brought about two expressions of God's amazing grace and mercy. *First*, my mind, speech, and intellectual abilities were not damaged and are functioning as crisply, clearly, and effectively as ever. *Second*, with the required new geographic location God has provided an ideal team member whose complementary credentials, skills, gifts, and abilities so compatibly fill essential needs for properly writing this book that without his work, the completion of the project would not have been possible. In fact, little did I realize how much I needed his expert involvement, but as I identify the multiple roles he has played so effectively for nearly a year, you will understand why he deserves special thanks for being available to God and desirous of undertaking these tasks. Let me tell you about him.

He is Dr. Tom Cragoe, whose credentials include a Th.M ('83) and a Th.D ('87) from Dallas Theological Seminary; twelve years in the pastorate ('84–'95); Associate Professor in the Theology Department of Moody Bible Institute ('95–2001); Associate Professor of Bible at Cedarville University (2001–'07); Professor of Bible & Theology at Summit University ('07–2015).

Our total Biblical, doctrinal and writing compatibility has created a natural climate for him to effectively consult, advise, suggest and make improvements in the style and flow of material as he applied his excellent literary and editing skills. Add computer ability (compensating for my computer illiteracy) to an indispensable list with the capability of formatting, footnoting, and preparing an excellent final manuscript. Among other positive benefits, include a new, deep and faithful friend and a persistent encourager, and we have a finished book that Dr. Cragoe and I trust and pray that God will be pleased to use in the experience of Christians willing to pursue godly living with contentment and a trustworthy stewardship of life.

CHAPTER 1

How Stewardship Responsibilities Change over Time

It is helpful to begin our discussion of stewardship by reflecting on the stark difference in the stewardship responsibilities designed by God for Israel and for the church in the New Testament. The nation of Israel (the physical descendants of Abraham) lived under the Mosaic Covenant (the Old Testament Law). That Old Testament Law guaranteed complete and absolute *prosperity and protection* over every nation of the world as long as Israel would diligently obey the Lord their God and be careful to do all His commandments (Deut. 28:1–14). In contrast, God promises the church to meet our basic *needs* and provide strength and sufficient grace through the permanently indwelling power of the Holy Spirit to endure suffering, persecution, opposition, and even martyrdom. Furthermore, the church is guaranteed a glorious deliverance from God's future Tribulation judgment "...when the Lord Himself will descend from heaven...and the dead in Christ shall rise first. Then we who are alive and remain will be caught up (raptured) together with them in the clouds to meet the Lord in the air, and so shall we ever be with the Lord (1 Thess. 4:16–17). As one prominent dispensational theologian writes, "Pretribulationism sees the Rapture as the next event on God's program."[1]

A steward is a person who receives delegated responsibility to manage something which belongs to his master. By virtue of His position as Creator, all creation is under God's authority (He is Lord over it, Ps. 24:1; Col. 1:16). As His subjects, God has appointed us as stewards of all He has created—whether material resources, talents and abilities, or time (Gen. 1:26–30). We are to carefully manage that which belongs to God (1 Cor. 4:2).

Rather than giving us all His instructions at one point in time, God chose to reveal the Bible in successive stages. In the progress of revelation, distinct stages (or stewardship arrangements) in the outworking of God's sovereign plan have become evident. Each distinct household arrangement is marked by God communicating specific responsibilities to humanity (stewardship obligations) by means of special revelation. For example, prior to the Fall, we find that Adam was created both innocent and with a positive holiness which enabled him to have face-to-face communication with God (Genesis 1:28—3:6). His main responsibilities were to be fruitful and multiply, to maintain the garden, and to not eat of the tree of the knowledge of good and evil (Gen. 1:28; 2:15–17). When Adam and Eve consciously disobeyed the revealed will of God, a change in stewardship arrangement occurred (Genesis 4:1—8:14). While humanity was still to multiply, that process would be accompanied by pain (Gen. 3:15). While humanity was still to exercise dominion over the earth, that

---

[1] Charles C. Ryrie, *What You Should Know About The Rapture* (Chicago, IL: Moody Press, 1981), 28-35.

task would be more difficult because the ground was cursed (Gen. 3:17–18). Because of Adam's sin, human nature was now corrupt (Eph. 2:3) and the race was subject to physical death (Rom. 5:12). Separation from God could only be removed by faith in the coming of a promised Deliverer (Gen. 3:15), demonstrated by bringing an acceptable blood sacrifice as God had taught them to do (Gen. 4:4).

Another clear illustration of distinct ways in which God ordered His household in identifiable stages is humanity's stewardship of food. In the garden of Eden, Adam and Eve ate fruit, grain, and vegetables (Gen. 2:15–16). Immediately following the flood, Noah was permitted to not only eat those kinds of food, but now was also permitted to eat meat, as long as it was not eaten with blood (Gen. 9:3). Under the Mosaic Law, God gave Israel specific instructions concerning unclean meat that was not to be eaten. For example, animals without cloven hoofs or which did not chew the cud were unclean (Lev. 11:3–8), as were sea creatures without scales or fins (Lev. 11:9–12) and birds of prey (Lev. 11:13–19). One indication that the church is distinct from Israel is the removal of these dietary regulations (Mark 7:19; Acts 10:14–15). Hence, during this dispensation, the church is no longer accountable as stewards of their food in the same manner that Israel was under the Mosaic Law.

In the progress of revelation, another distinct stewardship arrangement (or dispensation) is the Mosaic Law that extended until Pentecost (Acts 2:1). In this particular household arrangement, God as Master dealt specifically with the nation of Israel through the Mosaic Law. A Jewish person was saved by belief in the coming Deliverer (the Messiah, 1 Pet. 1:10–11). That saving faith was then demonstrated by obeying the Law—613 commandments covering all phases of life. It revealed in specific detail God's will in that economy (stewardship responsibilities).

The next stage in God's plan was the stewardship arrangement established at Pentecost and continuing to the Rapture, commonly identified as the church age. The New Testament is quite clear that the church did not exist in the Old Testament. It was a mystery (Eph. 3:1–12). It was a *new* creation (Eph. 2:15), formed by the baptism of the Holy Spirit (1 Cor. 12:13) and uniquely indwelled by the Spirit (John 14:16–17). During this dispensation, a person is saved by faith in Jesus Christ—the promised Deliverer (1 Cor. 15:1–11). When it comes to sanctification, the church is no longer under the Mosaic Law (Rom. 10:4). Rather, the church is under the law of Christ, experiences privileges that are unique to this age, and discharges stewardship responsibilities that are in keeping with God's plan for this particular era.

Is another book on stewardship necessary? This is a reasonable question since during the last six decades a number of books have been written about Christian stewardship. They're designed to cover at least some, if not all the biblical instructions about the subject. In fact, some of them are revised, expanded, and even rewritten efforts to adequately address one or more of the areas of stewardship in order to include (1) material resources (money and possessions), (2) talents and abilities, and (3) time, which all together represent the complete stewardship of life.

As Bible scholars, teachers, expositors and authors with (1) college and graduate level teaching and administrative experience, (2) extensive pastoral and local church leadership experience, (3) experience as a regional mission director (including recruitment, deputation, training and oversight experience), plus (4) tent making (contracting) business experience, we believe *The Christian's Complete Biblical Stewardship of Life* is a needed book. We are confident that it is appropriate and helpful for you, our readers, as a *complete* presentation designed to enable all Christians to know and experience *how members of the body of Christ should manage what really belongs to God.* This chapter presents just an overview of the subject that will be dealt with much more extensively throughout the book.

The above explanation makes it clear that we hold to a classic dispensational interpretive approach to the Scriptures. This is because

> it remains the most helpful tool for consistent, noncontradictory interpretation of Scripture.... The essence of dispensationalism, then, is (1) the distinction between Israel and the Church. (2) This grows out of the dispensationalist's consistent employment of normal or plain or historical grammatical interpretation, and (3) it reflects an understanding of the basic purpose of God in all His dealings with mankind as that of glorifying Himself through salvation and other purposes as well.[2]

When this interpretive approach is not followed consistently, it is easy to mistakenly arrive at the conclusion that the church should practice tithing in conjunction with

---

[2] Charles C. Ryrie, *Dispensationalism* (Chicago, IL: Moody Press, 1995), 11-12, 38, 41.

New Testament passages describing grace giving (1 Tim. 6:6–19; 1 Cor. 16:1–4; 2 Cor. 8:1—9:15). Examining two Old Testament passages should help us recognize the danger of allowing this to happen.

As Israel was preparing to enter the land God had promised to give them, Moses completed a review of the Law and preparation ceremonies for entrance (Deut. 4:44—27:28). He then speaks for God in the words of Deut. 28:1–14.

> Now it shall be, if you diligently obey the LORD your God, being careful to do all His commandments which I command you today, the LORD your God will set you high above all the nations of the earth.... Blessed *shall be* the offspring of your body and the produce of your ground and the offspring of your beasts, the increase of your herd and the young of your flock. Blessed *shall be* your basket and your kneading bowl.... The LORD will command the blessing upon you in your barns and in all that you put your hand to, and He will bless you in the land which the LORD your God gives you.... The LORD will make you abound in prosperity, in the offspring of your body and in the offspring of your beast and in the produce of your ground, in the land which the LORD swore to your fathers to give you. The LORD will open for you His good storehouse, the heavens, to give rain to your land in its season and to bless all the work of your hand; and you shall lend to many nations, but you shall not borrow....if you listen to the commandments of the LORD your God, which I charge you today, to observe *them* carefully, and do not turn aside from any of the words which I

command you today, to the right or to the left, to go after other gods to serve them.

It is clear that this is a guarantee from God to the nation of Israel of *complete and absolute prosperity, protection, and blessing* over every nation of the world as long as Israel would diligently obey the Lord their God and be careful to do all His commandments. This specific guarantee applies to Israel and should in no way be applied to the New Testament church.

About one-hundred years after the nation returned from captivity to Palestine, having rebuilt Jerusalem and the second Temple, they returned to their spiritual neglect of the true worship of the Lord. As a result, the Lord rebuked them by the prophet Malachi in the words recorded in Malachi 3:6–12.

> "For I, the LORD, do not change; therefore you, O sons of Jacob, are not consumed. From the days of your fathers you have turned aside from My statutes and have not kept *them.* Return to Me, and I will return to you," says the LORD of hosts. "But you say, 'How shall we return?' "Will a man rob God? Yet you are robbing Me! But you say, 'How have we robbed You?' In tithes and offerings. "You are cursed with a curse, for you are robbing Me, the whole nation *of you!* "Bring the whole tithe into the storehouse, so that there may be food in My house, and test Me now in this," says the LORD of hosts, "if I will not open for you the windows of heaven and pour out for you a blessing until it overflows. Then I will rebuke the devourer for you, so that it will not destroy the fruits of the ground; nor will your vine in

the field cast *its grapes*," says the LORD of hosts. "All the nations will call you blessed, for you shall be a delightful land," says the LORD of hosts.

Like the previous passage, Israel is identified as the recipient by the context of the book of Malachi and by being called "O sons of Jacob" (3:6) and "the whole nation of you" (3:9b). Consequently, the specific rebuke could only be directly applied to Israel and not to the New Testament church. However, numerous writers, by using an inconsistent approach to interpretation, have chosen to add some concept of tithing to New Testament grace giving.

Following this dispensational approach, a review of the more popular books on stewardship written over the last six decades and still available, reveals an absence of, or weakness in at least one or more of the following elements.

1. The first distinctive of our discussion is the approach to Scripture upon which it is based. As dispensational, this work consistently employs a literal, historical, grammatical interpretation of the Bible, which leads to acknowledging and consistently applying the distinction between Israel and the Church.[3]

---

[3] Interestingly, most of the suggested books on stewardship listed in Appendix C are not written from a classic dispensational perspective. Two helpful works that are written from that perspective are:

Charles C. Ryrie, *Balancing the Christian Life* (Chicago, IL: Moody Press, 1969).

Charles C. Ryrie, *Dispensationalism*, Revised and Expanded (Chicago, IL: Moody Press, 1995, 2007).

Another problem that appears on books about stewardship of material resources is the emphasis on tithing. Two books which mistakenly apply the Old Testament's teaching on tithing to the church are:

2. The Second distinctive element of our discussion is our recognition and application of the vital and unique role of the Holy Spirit in the church. Since the beginning of the church at Pentecost, the Spirit permanently indwells every member of the body of Christ and provides all needed power, direction, and enablement to believers as they seek to fulfill their stewardship responsibilities.

3. The third element is the importance of presenting the stewardship of life in a complete and thorough way. For example, many books only address the stewardship of material resources (money or possessions),[4] or the stewardship of time (time management).[5] Other books may address both, yet say little or nothing about the stewardship of talents and abilities.[6] Though none of the three areas of stewardship is more important

---

Stephen F. Olford, *The Grace Of Giving-A Biblical Study Of Christian Stewardship* Revised Edition (Grand Rapids, MI: Kregel Publications, 1972, 2000).

Charlie W. Shedd, *How To Develop A Tithing Church* (Nashville, TN: Abingdon Press, 1961).

[4] Three helpful resources on the specific subject of material resources are:
Gene A. Getz, *A Biblical Theology Of Material Possessions* (Chicago, IL: Moody Publishers, 1990).

Gene A. Getz, *Real Prosperity: Biblical Principles of Material Possessions* (Chicago, IL: Moody Publishers, 1990).

John Stott, *The Grace of Giving-Ten Principles of Giving* (Peabody, MA: Hendrickson Publishers, 2004).

[5] Two helpful resources on the specific subject of time management are:
Ted W. Engstrom and R. Alec Mackenzie, *Managing Your Time* (Grand Rapids, MI: Zondervan, 1967).

Charlie W. Shedd, *Time for All Things* (Nashville, TN: Abingdon Press, 1962).

[6] Two helpful resources that discuss both our stewardship of material resources and time are:

than any other, we are convinced that all three require nothing less than a total commitment to God and His will in order to be trustworthy stewards (1 Tim. 6:6–19). We are also persuaded that the perspective of godly living with contentment can be more readily grasped when all three areas of stewardship are united with teaching concerning the unique role of the Holy Spirit in the church (John 14:16–17;16:13–15; Acts 1:4–5, 8). For it is the Spirit's permanent indwelling that provides the source of power, enablement and direction for the believer during this age.

4. The fourth element is the need for a thorough,[7] clear, and practical presentation which includes all of the major related passages of the New Testament, communicated with detailed exposition and sound doctrinal teaching, designed to provide every reader with adequate precepts, principles, plus Spirit-led direction and enablement necessary to experience a complete and fulfilling trustworthy life of stewardship for the glory of God.

Alfred Martin, *Not My Own* (Chicago, IL: Moody Press, 1968). Also the revised reprint edition – Alfred Martin, *Biblical Stewardship* (Debuque, IA: ECS Ministries, revised 2005, reprinted 2010, 2014).

[7] One helpful work that is a *general* treatment of the stewardship of material resources and time is Kirk Nowery, *The Stewardship of Life* (Camarillo, CA: Spire Resources, Inc., Publishers, 2004).

CHAPTER 2

Stewardship of the Process:
God's design for the process of becoming

Our development as individuals is frequently described with familiar expressions like "We are now becoming what we are going to be." Such statements aptly describe the inescapable *process* every Christian experiences from the moment we are saved (or spiritually born) to the conclusion of our earthly existence by means of physical death or the Rapture (1 Thess. 4:13–16; 1 Cor. 15:51–58). That span encompasses our total Christian life, including our physical, mental, and spiritual growth and development, as well as the controllable and uncontrollable, positive and negative events in our lives, all that cause us to continually experience change. For us as Christians, the word *process* is particularly descriptive, since our lives are constantly subjected to whatever changes in circumstances God may allow, so that by our submissive response to Him and His will we are and become what He wants us to be for His glory.

Its original form, "We are now becoming what we are going to be," ties the present together with the future. With a slight twist it ties the present with the past as we say,

"We now are what we have become." This added dimension completes a helpful perspective for assessing how much positive progress we have made in the past *process* in order to determine what we should do in the future. In other words, it helps us determine whether or not we are maintaining an acceptable pace in our pursuit of becoming what God wants us to be. Though we cannot change it, our past is an important tool that we should use in making our assessment. It enables us (1) to identify any weaknesses, deficiencies and mistakes, (2) to make necessary immediate adjustments, and (3) to determine and refine a future course of action designed to keep us focused on the goal of being and becoming what God wants us to be. The value of such regularly repeated assessments will become even more apparent as our study examines and applies the truth of Scripture that explains "experiencing the Biblical Stewardship of Life," which really amounts to "managing what really belongs to God with godliness and contentment."

Being or becoming what God wants us to become does not happen easily, quickly, or by accident. In fact, both Satan (God's archenemy) who controls the world system, as well as the flesh within us, opposes our becoming what God wants us to be with every possible hindrance and obstacle. Even though Satan is powerful and persistent, God can enable us to defeat him "because greater is He who is in you [us] than he who is in the world" (1 John 4:4)—so take heart! And since we have reason to assume that, as readers of our book you seriously desire to understand and pursue a biblical stewardship of life, we also believe it is imperative for us to take time and space at this point in our presentation to identify and explain two companion challenges of an effectively designed and well established opposition strategy that Satan (our enemy) has already created and put in place to frustrate and defeat us from experiencing our stewardship goal.

The first challenge of this strategy is the reality that during the last thirty to fifty years, the Satanically-controlled, secular world system has creatively caused America to become a more affluent and ungodly culture than we could have ever imagined.

In a chapter entitled, "The New Moral (Dis)Order," nationally known pastor Robert Jeffress asks, "How did we get so far off track?" Billy Graham offers this persuasive answer: The fact that moral and spiritual decadence is upon us today becomes more evident at every turn of our daily newspaper. We live in a day when old values are rejected and the sense of significance and purpose has disappeared from many people's lives. Yes, we need to cry out to be saved – saved from ourselves, for it is the soul of a nation and a culture that is dying! The world is on a moral binge such as was not known even in the days of Rome. We have at our fingertips every pleasure that man is capable of enjoying, and man has abused every gift God ever gave him, including sex, until he no longer finds joy and satisfaction in them.[8]

Here is an amazing fact. Those quotes come from a book entitled *World Aflame* that was published in 1965. If those things were true over a half-century ago, how much more do those words describe our world today?

Undeniably, America is now a culture where greed, excessive drug and alcohol use, gay rights, same sex marriage, and legalized abortion have become acceptable practices, to

---

[8] Taken from Robert Jeffress, *Countdown to the Apocalypse* (New York, NY, Faith Words, 2015), 79-80.

mention only a few. Along with all of this ungodly activity has come extreme moral and spiritual decay at the hands of the selfish pursuit of godless independence, self-gratifying prosperity, insatiable pleasure, and avoidance of pain. Not only does the worldly system make this all appear so important and attractive to the lust and desires of non-Christians, but most Christians really struggle with the accessibility of things we've come to think will satisfy us. The end result is that our love for God and our serious commitment to His will wane and often disappear from the priority list in our relationship with God. These distractions distort the clarity of what is godly and really important. In addition, the secular system's handling of charitable financial matters has unfortunately led the well-meaning majority of doctrinally sound churches and Christian organizations to adopt fund raising and development methods and techniques that are actually contrary to the doctrinal teachings of Scripture for the church (see 1 Tim. 6:6–19). Be assured, we will consistently endeavor to provide greater awareness of this opposition, as well as godly direction and insights for effectively meeting this challenge.

The second challenge of the opposition strategy of Satan is inseparably related to first. It is identified as Biblical illiteracy. This companion challenge is a huge obstacle to the spiritual growth and effective ministry of the body of Christ. It must be acknowledged and confronted by committed Christians to apply strong determination and godly disciplines that the indwelling Holy Spirit has promised to provide as we submit to His enablement (John 14:26; 16:13–15). An excellent book addressing this subject entitled, *Taking Back the Good Book* should be read or reviewed by every Christian to discover how damaging this challenge is to the spiritual vitality of

Bible believing individuals, families and churches. The author, Woodrow Kroll, says "America faces a great crisis: The Book [the Bible] that has played an integral role in developing and forming our great nation is now the same Book that few read and even fewer understand."[9] He goes on to say,

> But the Book so many love is not the book so many read. In fact, Bible reading has declined sharply over the years. And so has Bible knowledge. What the assaults of liberal theologians...and the attacks of atheists couldn't do, now Satan...seeks to accomplish through simple neglect. Today, we face a real crisis: Biblical illiteracy.[10]

For our ability to resist being a part of the crisis Kroll writes,

> So what is Bible literacy? Is it just reading the Bible? No, it's more. Reading is fundamental, but it isn't enough. You have to read the Bible and then interpret it and apply it to your life. Those are the initial steps in Biblical literacy. They are also the first steps toward spiritual maturity.[11]

So we must not only accept responsibility for developing disciplines that enable us to personally grow in Biblical literacy, but also to determine whether our local churches

---

[9] Woodrow Kroll, *Taking Back the Good Book* (Wheaton, IL: Good News Publishers, 2007), flyleaf.
[10] Kroll, 11-12.
[11] Kroll, 58.

are addressing the challenge as well. For you see, the same reliable Christian surveys and research that reveal the Biblical illiteracy of individuals also clearly shows us that a growing number of Bible-believing local churches, both large and small, are actually contributing to the problem. In fact, notice Kroll's comment about the extent of the church's dilemma when he states, "Biblical illiteracy is not *a* problem in the church. Biblical illiteracy is *the* problem in the church."[12] Steven Lawson's excellent book entitled, *Famine in the Land* is written for the specific purpose of exposing and dealing with this problem. His subtitle "A Passionate Call For Expository Preaching" clearly identifies the root cause. Lawson quotes from J. I. Packer's definition of expository preaching, "The true idea of preaching is that the preacher should become a mouthpiece for the text, opening it up and applying it as a word from God to his hearers, talking only that the text itself and speak and be heard."[13] Then Lawson adds, "It is the man of God opening the Word of God and expounding its truths so that the voice of God may be heard, the glory of God seen, and the will of God obeyed."[14]

That kind of preaching and teaching was precisely how the church's foundational work of the apostles was accomplished from the moment the Holy Spirit founded the Church by permanently indwelling every believer on the day of Pentecost (Acts 2) and Peter, John and the apostles began to teach and preach "and that day there were added about three thousand souls. They were continually devoting themselves

---

[12] Kroll, 79.
[13] Steven J. Larson, *Famine in the Land: A Passionate Call for Expository Preaching* (Chicago, IL: Moody Publishers, 2003), 18.
[14] Larson, 18.

to the apostles teaching" (Acts 2:41b–42a). Then Lawson adds, "In this God designated role, the apostles spoke divine revelation to the church. Thus the church's ministry would be 'built on the foundation of the apostles and prophets' (Eph. 2:20)."[15] Lawson continues,

> By the end of the first century, the apostles teaching was permanently recorded in the 27 books of the New Testament...either written by...or backed by an apostle.... Everyone and everything in the church must yield to that New Testament authority. Every decision, direction, practice, ministry, attitude, and motive must be brought into conformity with their instruction.[16]

In contrast to God's New Testament design, Lawson then describes the opposition strategy.

> As the church advances into the 21st century the stress to produce booming ministries has never been greater.... Sad to say, the pressure...has led many ministries to sacrifice the centrality of biblical preaching on the altar of man-centered pragmatism... exposition is being replaced with entertaining, doctrine with drama, and theology with theatrics. The pulpit, once the focal point of the church, is now being overshadowed by a variety of church-growth techniques.[17]

---

[15] Larson, 40.
[16] Larson, 41.
[17] Larson, 25.

He concludes by saying, "Doing God's work in God's way requires an unwavering commitment to feeding people God's Word through relentless biblical preaching and teaching."[18]

In completing this description of Satan's modern day difficult challenges, we want to assure you that this book has been written with our firm, unwavering commitment to teach God's Word through relentless biblical exposition. We are confident that by doing it God's way we can enable you to understand and experience God's good, acceptable, and perfect will as trustworthy stewards. In the process all of us can experience godliness with contentment while Satan is defeated and God receives all the glory that belongs to Him.

Not only is being or becoming what God wants us to become viciously attacked by Satan today, but most of the exemplary individuals in the Bible lived in some of the most unlikely and difficult spiritual environments—like the experiences of Noah, Job, Joseph, Moses, and Daniel, just to mention a few. We have selected one amazing and inspiring example for consideration, yet this person happens to be one of the lesser known biblical characters. But the biblical record of His experience reveals a complete, basic, workable, and essential formula in such clear, concise, and simple terms that it can be reduced to this single verse: *Ezra continued to become what God wanted him to be because, "Ezra had set his heart to study the law of the Lord and to practice it, and to teach His statutes and ordinances in Israel" (Ezra 7:10).*

In order to get a clearer picture of Ezra and his experiences we need to consider some details of his personal background

---

[18] Larson, 27.

and the responsibility that God had sovereignly designed for him. It is important first to understand that Ezra was born, reared, and became a man as an alien and an exiled member of the nation of Israel in Babylon. It was under those unfavorable conditions that he committed himself to God and the disciplined formula that enabled Ezra to become what God wanted him to be as a "scribe, skilled in the law of Moses, which the Lord God of Israel had given" (7:6a). This happened because Ezra determined to do precisely what God, through Moses, had told the entire nation of Israel to do a thousand years earlier in these words: "Now it shall be, if you will diligently obey the Lord your God, being careful to do all the commandments which I command you today, the Lord your God will set you high above all the nations of the earth" (Deut. 28:1). The following verses (28:2-13) describe incredible promised blessings that would accompany obedience. But the text continues with these words: "and do not turn aside from any of the words which I command you today.... But if it shall come about, if you will not obey the Lord your God... all these curses [listed in 28:16–68] shall come upon you and overtake you" (Deut. 28:14–15).

The sad story of history reveals that in spite of periods of obedience and rich blessing, the practice of the nation of Israel was dominated with repeated disobedience by wicked kings, religious leaders and the people, plus the ungodly splitting of the nation and God's judgment of the Northern Kingdom by means of the Assyrian captivity and subsequent international dispersion. Finally, the Southern Kingdom, including Judah and Jerusalem, was conquered for judgment through God's sovereignly designed Babylonian captivity concluding with Nebuchadnezzar's destruction of Jerusalem and the Temple. Even during and after the seventy-year captivity, the majority of the Israelites continued to walk in disobedience, remaining in Babylon, refusing to return to rebuild their Temple and city of Jerusalem when permitted, and blaming God for their plight. And it was into this corrupt spiritual environment and among these disobedient people that Ezra rose to leadership prominence spiritually and governmentally by means of his personal commitment to become the man God wanted Him to be.

Now that we have a picture of Ezra's ministry environment, as well as the challenges facing him, we need to explore the formula by which he lived. His effective ministry accomplishments are explained by the repeated phrase, "because the good hand of his God was upon him" (7:6, 9, 28; 8:18, 22, 31). Ezra 7:6–9 describes a successful nine-hundred mile journey from Babylon to Jerusalem. It lasted exactly four months and included about five thousand people whom Ezra had taught, motivated, enlisted, and led. Note that it says "the king granted him all he requested *because the hand of the Lord his God was upon him*" (7:6). Ezra points out God's sovereign role in the king's decree (7:12–26) as he thanks Him with these words:

> Blessed be the Lord, the God of our fathers, who has put such a thing as this in the king's heart...and to extend loving kindness to me before the king and his counselors and before all the king's mighty princes. Thus I was strengthened according to the hand of the Lord my God upon me, and I gathered leading men from Israel to go up with me" (7:27–28).

The phrase is applied again (7:9), this time to explain the successful four month journey. Then, the following verse (7:10) continues the narrative and gives us the reason why the "good hand of His God was upon him," in recognition of his effectiveness in service. Changing the first word, "for," to "because" (7:10, an acceptable translation) makes it a bit easier to understand how Ezra's applied life-style formula consistently elicited God's favor. It reads, "the good hand of his God was upon him because Ezra had set his heart to study the law of the Lord, and to practice it, and to teach His statutes and ordinances in Israel" (7:9b-10).

There's the formula we want to examine because it clearly reveals that "the key to Ezra's ministry was undoubtedly his resolute determination to learn, live, and proclaim the Scriptures.... It was Ezra's all-absorbing commitment to the Scriptures that enabled him to impact his generation."[19] The first thing it tells us that Ezra did was, "Ezra had set his heart" (7:10), that we will refer to as his

Prepared Heart

Which means that Ezra purposed in his heart, or *prepared his heart*, as the foundational step supporting everything else in his formula. In other words, we can declare that Ezra became what God wanted him to become because he was driven by determination or propelled by a purpose! If we are inclined to question the importance of his *prepared heart*, we need only to turn to the account of Solomon's ungodly son Rehoboam who, at the age of forty began to reign as king of

---

[19] Lawson, 83-84.

Judah, the Southern Kingdom of Israel and played a major role in splitting the United Kingdom of Israel into the Northern and Southern Kingdoms. In fact Rehoboam's wickedness is negatively described with the identical terminology as Ezra's righteousness: "He [Rehoboam] did evil *because he did not set [or prepare] his heart to seek the Lord*" (2 Chron. 12:14).

What a contrast between Rehoboam's behavior and the description given to Daniel as a teenager. When subjected to the pressures of Babylonian culture, he "made up his mind that he would not defile himself with the king's choice food or with the wine which he drank" (Dan. 1:8), and God honored his commitment with miraculous protection and governmental leadership. It also reminds us of Paul's impassioned appeal for our once-for-all dedication to God and His will in Romans 12:1–2, which Paul immediately follows with a directive for us to engage in the "transformation process by the renewing of our minds" (v. 2).

Since this transformational process clearly involves the intense study of biblical truth that enables us to "prove what the will of God is, that which is good and acceptable and perfect" (v. 2b), it is understandable why Ezra's prepared heart would give priority to

Pursue the Truth

"For Ezra had set his heart [prepared heart] to study the law of the Lord [pursue the truth]" (Ezra 7:10). The importance of his action is conveyed in Ezra's vocabulary because the Hebrew word for "study" represents so much more than casual reading. It is biblical exposition which Lawson adequately describes, "Thus, Ezra studied the Word by carefully searching it, investigating its truths, probing its parts, surveying its whole, striving to understand its meaning, being concerned to grasp its message. He was not content to skim the surface and gain a superficial knowledge of the text."[20] Another scholar adds this insightful perspective, "The Bible is the greatest of all books, to study it is the noblest of all pursuits; to understand it, the highest of all goals."[21] This kind of intense search for knowledge and wisdom is called for so frequently all throughout the Scriptures it was difficult to narrow our selection to the four following examples that confirm Ezra's formula.

After commending the Colossian congregation for their spiritual growth displayed by faith, hope, and love following their conversion, Paul encourages them to continue pressing on with these words:

> For this reason also...we have not ceased to pray for you and to ask that you may be filled with the knowledge [literally be filled full with the full knowledge] of His will in all spiritual wisdom and understanding, so that you will walk worthy of the Lord, to please Him in all respects...bearing fruit...and increasing in the knowledge of God; strengthened with all power... joyously giving thanks to the Father. (Col. 1:9–12).

This first example precisely describes what Ezra was doing as he engaged in weeks, months, even years of diligent, disciplined, and intensive study to know and understand

---

[20] Lawson, 87.
[21] Charles C. Ryrie, "To the Reader," in *The Ryrie Study Bible* (Chicago, IL: Moody Press, 1978), v.

God as "the Lord who exercises loving kindness, justice and righteousness on earth for He delights in these things" (Jer. 9:24). In other words, he was becoming skilled in *pursuing the truth* through essential research and development as business and industry does in order to produce the most effective product. Can we afford to do any less?

The second example is composed of a few verses that summarize all of Paul's exhortations to Timothy regarding his efforts to *pursue the truth*: "Be *diligent* to present yourself approved to God as a workman who does not need to be ashamed, accurately handling the word of truth" (2 Tim. 2:15). There could be no question regarding the time, energy and effort required to achieve this objective. Then Paul adds the following to impress upon Timothy both the value of the Book and the purpose for diligently studying with: "All Scripture is inspired by God and profitable for teaching, for reproof, for correction, for training in righteousness; so that the man of God may be equipped for every good work" (2 Tim. 3:16–17).

Anyone pursuing godly living with contentment soon recognizes that just as proper food is essential to the healthy physical development of man, accurate knowledge of the truth is essential to the healthy spiritual development of the spiritual man. That's why Peter says, "Like newborn babies, long for the pure milk of the word, so that by it you may grow in respect to salvation" (1 Pet. 2:2). The "pure milk of the word" in this context is not used in contrast to "solid food" as in Hebrews 5:12. Instead it includes all of the Word of God as the perfect diet to satisfy the appetite that "longs for" it and needs it for healthy growth and maturity. Furthermore, nothing can more effectively fortify our minds and hearts against the enticement of the affluent, ungodly American culture empowered by the world, the flesh, and Satan, all committed to exposing our minds to everything that is contrary to God and His truth.

Our fourth and final example is expressed in a couple statements Christ made in the Upper Room just before the crucifixion. They demonstrate that Ezra had the proper order when his *prepared heart* placed *pursue the truth* ahead of any other part of his formula. Christ said "If you love Me, you will keep my commandments" (John 14:15). He added "He who has My commandments and keeps them is the one who loves Me.... If anyone loves Me, he will keep My word...and the word which you hear is not Mine, but the Father's who sent Me" (John 14:21a, 23a, 24b). Just as it would be impossible to design an airplane without knowledge of aerodynamics, it is impossible for us to express our love for Christ by keeping His commandments without seriously studying the Scriptures in order to know what they are.

Unquestionably, Ezra's decision to *pursue the truth* was correctly placed in a priority position, but his formula did not stop there. Our key passage tells us that Ezra did "study the law of the Lord" (Ezra 7:10), but he also made certain to

Practice the Truth

Ezra not only had knowledge of the precepts, principles, and promises of the Word of God, but he also put them into practice. He was more than a spectator, he became a participant. Ezra knew firsthand the damage and disastrous results of (1) not knowing the truth, (2) not obeying the truth, (3) not applying the truth, and (4) ignoring the truth. Israel was experiencing the judgment that resulted from centuries of practicing those sins. He knew that ignorance of the truth is bad enough, but the sin of knowing and not doing it is deadly. Biblical history shows how it has repeatedly crippled, neutralized and generally damaged any positive impact of Israel's testimony for the glory of God in the Old Testament. The same could be said for Christianity's testimony for the glory of God since the beginning of the church. In spite of God's warnings and history's reminders, we see the threads of this deadly sin continuing.

For example, while Israel was waiting to go into the land that God would give them, Moses said,

> when the Lord your God brings you into the land which He swore to your fathers...to give you, great and splendid cities which you did not build, and houses full of good things which you did not fill, and hewn cisterns which you did not dig, vineyards and olive trees you did not plant...then *watch yourself, that you do not forget the Lord* who brought you from the land of Egypt. (Deut. 6:10–12, emphasis added)

And we know that as a nation they continued to forget God and pursue idolatry and immorality until God judged with captivity.

Ironically, about eight hundred and fifty years later the Lord spoke to the prophet Ezekiel about how his preaching was being received by some of the same captive exiles to whom Ezra ministered. The Lord said,

> They come to you as people come, and sit before you as My people and *hear your words, but they do not do*

them.... Behold, you are to them like a sensual song by one who has a beautiful voice and plays well on and instrument; for *they hear your words but they do not practice them.* (Ezek. 33:32–34, emphasis added)

In spite of warnings and judgments, this deadly sin persisted to the extent that there was urgent need to sternly address it only fifteen to twenty years after the beginning of the Church when the Holy Spirit came to permanently indwell every Christian on the day of Pentecost. As James thoroughly deals with the sin of not practicing the truth, he covers the essentials of Ezra's formula so effectively that we will conclude our *practice the truth* section with James exhortation:

But *prove yourselves doers of the word, and not merely hearers who delude themselves.* For if anyone is a hearer of the word and not a doer, he is like a man who looks at his natural face in a mirror; for once he has looked at himself and gone away, he has immediately forgotten what kind of person he was. But one who looks intently at the perfect law, the law, of liberty, and abides by it, not having become a forgetful hearer but an effectual doer, this man will be blessed in what he does. (James 1:22–25, emphasis added)

When we employ this kind of strong commitment to *practice the truth*, we, like Ezra, become qualified and motivated to

Proclaim the Truth

No one could have been more aware of the tremendous needs of the captive and exiled nation of Israel than Ezra who had spent his entire life in that very environment. The more he studied and practiced the law of the Lord, the more convinced he became that the people among whom he lived and to whom God had called him to minister, desperately needed to hear him "teach His statutes and ordinances in Israel" (Ezra 7:10c). This is what happens when we know and practice the living Word of God; *we just can't keep it to ourselves*. Ezra was compelled to share it because (1) he was continuing to learn it, (2) to practice it, and (3) he knew that this was Israel's only hope if they were going to glorify God by (a) repopulating Judah and Jerusalem, (b) finishing the rebuilding of the city and walls of Jerusalem (c) and spiritually reviving and reforming Israel in the land.

The first qualification for teaching is that *he who would teach must first know the subject. W*e are confident that Ezra was especially well qualified because "...he was a scribe skilled in the law of Moses" (Ezra 7:6a). The second qualification is that *he who would teach must practice what he knows.* Ezra was highly regarded for leadership because he effectively demonstrated in his life what he knew ("...the king granted all he requested because the hand of the Lord his God was upon him," Ezra 7:6b).

By applying his biblical formula for becoming godly, Ezra became the agent for accomplishing God's sovereignly designed tasks, and so can we. Since this represents a process, Ezra continued to become God's agent for numerous future tasks by consistently applying this formula. In reality we are always in the process of becoming—*we are now becoming what we are going to be.* We know Ezra experienced this in spite of unlikely and difficult spiritual conditions, as many others have done like Job, Joseph, and Daniel. Most of us, however, can experience this by simply employing the disciplines of the formula and do so without significant opposition or difficulty.

We need to understand that from God's perspective, regardless of the level of difficulty over which He has absolute control, the experiences are of equal importance for each participant. Psalm 139 clearly implies that it is *no less* essential for each one of us to apply Ezra's formula than it was for Ezra to do the same. For the psalm explains that in eternity past, God sovereignly ordained people, circumstances and responses in keeping with His predetermined will. This is explained by the words, "Your eyes have seen my unformed substance, and in Your book were all written the days that were ordained for me, when as yet there was not one of them" (Ps. 139:16). In fact, what we may call accidents, mistakes, or uncontrollable events, including circumstances and conditions over which pagan world rulers, powers, and even Satan himself appear to dominate, are all circumscribed by our almighty, sovereign, creator, and loving God. The ultimate objective is that all of these experiences are designed to bring glory to God and defeat our powerful enemies while we are abundantly blessed to be trustworthy stewards whose talents and abilities God uses to orchestrate our becoming something He wants us to be. These are the joys of experiencing godly living with contentment.

As we conclude this chapter on *the process of becoming,* we want to share with you the account of one of the most dramatic and inspiring examples of a godly person living a life of becoming what God wants us to become. Her name is Fanny Crosby, the writer of numerous familiar hymns. She was born on March 24, 1820 in Putnam County, New York and lived to be 95. Six weeks after her birth Fanny became ill with an eye infection and a doctor's careless treatment left her blind for life. Her father died that same year, making it necessary for her mother to support the family by working as a maid. Fanny was raised by her godly grandmother and mother who provided a strong Christian environment.

As early as possible they began to read to Fanny from the Bible. They soon discovered that she had a voracious appetite and amazing capacity to memorize (as much as five chapters in a week). She also had a love of poetry that was accompanied by an ability to write and think in poetic verse. For example, this poem is identified by many as her first and was written when she was eight years old. As you read it, notice her attitude about her life and her blindness:

> Oh, what a happy child I am
> Although I cannot see!
> I am resolved that in this world
> Contented I will be.

> How many blessings I enjoy
> That others people don't,
> To weep and sigh because I'm blind
> I cannot, and I won't!

It was obvious that she possessed an unusually high level of intelligence, and at age fifteen, Fanny received a placement in the recently founded New York Institute for the Blind where she spent twelve years as a student and eleven years as a teacher. It was during this time that she greatly enriched her professional skills in poetry and music.

One of the most memorable events of her life story took place when Fanny was ten years old. Her mother took her on a boat trip down the Hudson River to New York City to an eye specialist to see if anything could possibly be done about her blindness. When she arrived back home she wrote a letter to her grandfather telling him about the experience. She told him about the boat and the river and then described all that she sensed and felt about the tall buildings in the city. She explained the visit with the doctor, indicating that he was certain nothing could be done for her eyes, about which she commented, "That's OK grandfather, God knows all about it!"

Then Fanny described the trip home and closed the letter by saying "That's all for now, Love, Fanny." But then she added a P. S. that read:

> Grandfather, I don't think I've told you, but my mother says I can recite the first four books of the Old Testament and the first four books of the New Testament, and I don't make one mistake. Do you think God could use a little blind girl like me?

We're certain you know the answer. At ten years of age Fanny was already becoming what she was going to be for God. During her lifetime she wrote more than five thousand hymns and became one of the most prolific writers of gospel hymns in American history. It is reported that one publishing company has hundreds of Fanny's poems in their files just waiting to be set to music. As we would expect, her hymns and books of poetry are especially dependable for biblical accuracy. Many of Fanny's hymns refer to *seeing*, which is particularly significant since she experienced her first physical sight in 1915 when she passed from this life into the presence of Christ.

A closing quote tells us volumes about Fanny Crosby's spiritual maturity.

> The doctor who destroyed her sight never forgave himself and moved from the area, but Fanny Crosby held no ill will toward him. "If I could meet him now," she wrote, "I would say 'Thank you, thank you' –over and over again—for making me blind."[22]

In fact, she claimed that if she could have her sight restored, she would not attempt it. She felt that her blindness was God's gift to her so that she could write songs for His glory. "I could not have written thousands of hymns," she said, "if I had been hindered by the distractions of seeing all the interesting and beautiful objects that would have been presented to my notice."[23]

Throughout her life Fanny Crosby continued to become what God wanted her to be. As a result, for generations to come she will remain an exceptional example of what it really means to be a trustworthy steward of her incredible talents and abilities, time, and material resources for God's glory.

Since *all of us are now becoming what we are going to be*, let's make certain it's what God wants us to be!

---

[22] Warren W. Wiersbe, *50 People Every Christian Should Know* (Grand Rapids, MI: Baker Books, 2009), 102.
[23] Wiersbe, 102.

CHAPTER 3

Stewardship of the Scriptures (Part 1): God's design for handling the Scriptures

Our Commitment

This work is committed to *Biblical accuracy*—the belief that the Bible is God's only truth provided in written form to and for humanity. Consequently, we have sought to make certain that everything written in this book is in complete harmony with what the Lord has recorded in His Book.

Our Objective

Godly living with contentment is not only contained in the subtitle of this book, but it represents our objective for writing it. The contents are intended to explain all that the title suggests.

> Godliness with contentment is the basic necessity of the Christian life. No matter what else a man has, unless he has this, he has only a superstructure

without a foundation. In His children's hearts the Lord wants first of all to find godliness with contentment.[24]

The following four points describe more specifically how that subject will be developed.

First, ever since the church was founded by God on the day of Pentecost and the Holy Spirit began His unique ministry of permanently indwelling every member of the body of Christ, all Christians have been able to experience *godly living* by committing their lives completely to God and engaging in the ongoing process of transformation that enables them to know and experience the good, acceptable, and perfect will of God. This essential, life changing commitment is described in Romans 12:1–5, and it provides the key to the continual pursuit of godly living and the Holy Spirit's direction, control, and enablement. Notice at this opening point, we have purposely used descriptive expressions like *"can be experienced," "ongoing process,"* and *"continual pursuit"* to identify the concept of godly living as an active, transformational, growing and maturing lifestyle, punctuated by positive stages of progressive development and impact for the glory of God. God's design for *the process of becoming* has been chosen for the subtitle of our first chapter to establish our focus on this vital aspect of godly living that will be frequently referred to in the book by the phrase *"We are now becoming what we are going to be."*

Second, the phrase *with contentment* comes directly from I Timothy 6:6. The entire sixth chapter of Paul's letter to Timothy contains excellent guidance for Christians desiring to practice

---

[24] Charles C. Ryrie, *Balancing the Christian Life* (Chicago, IL: Moody Press, 1969), 95.

trustworthy stewardship of their material resources in a godly manner while experiencing true, biblical contentment. As a result, this passage will be discussed in detail in order to challenge Christians to exercise the proper stewardship of their material resources. It must be emphasized that we have placed this area of stewardship in our presentation's priority position because we must all deal with our dominant, ungodly, affluent American culture. For this current culture is increasingly infecting, confusing, and crippling us as Christians and evangelical congregations, while perpetuating destructive, immoral and ungodly behavior in our decaying secular society. To underscore the looming impact of this secular culture that is conceived and propagated by the Satanically controlled world system, we must pause to observe a prominent Christian historian's description:

Among its many manifestations are these:

1. *A trivialization of values.* This flows from our consumerism, the gathering of wealth, and a preoccupation with sports and leisure. Americans live for the tantalization of mere pleasures, while public virtues crumble into the abyss of private, individual values.
2. *Self-absorption and self-centered living.* As monitored by our social conversations, we seem to value athleticism (the virtue of strength), physical beauty (the art of temporal attractiveness), and money (portfolios and retirement packages) above everything, not concern or sacrifice for others.
3. *A loss of thankfulness.* Preoccupied with ourselves, we have lost the grace of being thankful. It is sad to live

in a world where there is no one to thank because we ourselves have become the cause and source of all good things.[25]

And our pause also needs to include the Apostle Paul's similar description of the last days:

> But realize this, that in the last days difficult times will come, for man will be lovers of self, lovers of money, boastful, arrogant, revilers, disobedient to parents, ungrateful, unholy, unloving, irreconcilable, malicious gossips, without self-control, brutal, haters of good, treacherous, reckless, conceited, lovers of pleasure rather than lovers of God, holding to a form of godliness, although they have denied its power; avoid such men as these. (2 Tim. 3:1-5)

Third, while there certainly is no question that the stewardship of material resources in the godly Christian's life is important, one's stewardship of talents and time are equally important. Since all three are similarly impacted and interrelated by the same foundational principles, all three should be carried out in the same godly manner with contentment. To do otherwise creates an unhealthy imbalance in our Christian experience.

Fourth, in light of the urgency discussed in our second point above, the stewardship of material resources has been selected as the first area of stewardship to be dealt with in our discussion. 1 Timothy 6:1–19 is a key portion of the Bible

---

[25] John D. Hannah, *How Do We Glorify God?* (Phillipsburg, NJ: P & R Publishing, 2000), 7.

dealing with the stewardship of material resources. Our objective is to clearly and accurately present God's solution to the challenge we all are facing, while pointing out the current issues created by this culture, so that we can experience godly living (including our stewardship of material resources) with contentment now.

Our Methodology

There are at least five ways that the biblical accountability of our discussion is reflected in this book:

First, Biblical content is extensively used throughout this book. Passages from the Bible are directly and indirectly quoted, as well as explained.[26] Summary biblical concepts and precepts are clearly stated.

Second, we believe that the literal, grammatical, historical method of Biblical interpretation is the most reliable method for determining the accurate meaning of the entire Bible.

Third, this work will seek to provide accurate Biblical definitions of key concepts. These definitions will appear in the form of precise and clear descriptions of the terminology, concepts, and doctrines found in the passages under investigation.

Fourth, biblical precepts will be identified as they appear throughout the Bible. Precepts are commands or directives given by God as rules for moral action or conduct. They are usually clear and simple, and tell us what God wants us to do. While precepts are a large part of New Testament writings specifically directed to the Church, they are more commonly

---

[26] All quotations of the Bible are from the *New American Standard Version* unless otherwise indicated.

found in the Old Testament, directed to Israel living under the Mosaic Law. The Mosaic Law contains over 613 ordinances, statues, and judgments, addressing virtually every aspect of individual and corporate activity for the nation of Israel. There are also New Testament precepts that are directed specifically to the church in a normative way.

One example of precepts that are directed to the church in the New Testament is found in 1 Thessalonians 5:16–18, which states, "Rejoice always. Pray without ceasing, in everything give thanks, for this is God's will for you in Christ Jesus." The required response to God's precepts is obedience, with no need for special wisdom or prayer for discernment. To help us grasp what such precepts involve, look at it this way. When our heavenly Father commands, His child is expected to obey in faith, believing that his Father, the sovereign God of the universe, can bring about results that will both benefit His child and glorify the Father. Our obedience to such precepts will cause praise, thanksgiving and wonder.

Fifth, Biblical principles will be identified. A principle is a foundational law concerning moral standards of conduct upon which others are based. It is broader than a precept in that the interpreter must bridge the gap from the biblical to the modern audience. Any given biblical passage has one meaning—that which the author intended to communicate in the text. A principle has an application of that meaning to the church today. In developing principles, one must have a reliable method to make sure that the applications are within the boundaries established by the biblical author's meaning for the passage. The New Testament was specifically written to provide principles that guide and direct both congregations and individuals regarding productive godly living with contentment.

The following chapter identifies seven major principles that are foundational to the Christian's biblical call to godly living with contentment and to our fulfillment of trustworthy stewardship.

CHAPTER 4

Stewardship of the Scriptures (Part 2): God's foundational Stewardship principles

1. The Principle of Ownership: *God's Ownership*

Since God created the heavens and the earth, He is the owner of everything. Psalm 24:1 states, "The earth is the Lord's, and all it contains, the world, and those who dwell in it." God Himself declares, "whatever is under the whole heaven is mine" (Job 41:17). Only when we believe and submit to God's ownership can we experience all God's good, acceptable, and perfect will promises for both this life now and for eternity.

2. The Principle of Stewardship: *God's Requirement*

Scripture consistently presents the idea that God is the sovereign Ruler (or Master) over His subjects (or household). As His subjects, God has appointed humankind as stewards of all He has created and entrusted to us—whether material resources, talents and abilities, or time (Gen. 1:26–30). As stewards, we are to carefully manage that which belongs to God. As God exercises His sovereign rule, distinguishable economies[27] (distinct household arrangements or dispensations) become evident in the outworking of God's purpose.[28] In each dispensation, God communicates specific responsibilities to humankind (stewardship obligations) by means of special revelation. This present church age is a distinct household arrangement in the outworking of God's purpose. It was a mystery not revealed in the Old Testament (Eph. 3:4–9; Col. 1:26–27) that is distinct from Israel (Eph. 2:13–22). Built upon the revelatory foundation of the apostles and New Testament prophets (Eph. 2:20), the church began

---

[27] *"Economy*...suggests that certain features of different dispensations might be the same or similar....in the different economies of God's running the affairs of this world certain features are similar. However, the word *distinguishable* in the definition points out that some features are distinctive to each dispensation and mark them off from each other as different dispensations. These are contained in the particular revelation distinctive to each dispensation." C. Ryrie, *Dispensationalism* (Chicago: Moody Press, 1995), 28-29.

[28] This idea is central to the system of theology called dispensationalism. C. I. Scofield writes:

> The dispensations are a progressive and connected revelation of God's dealings with men, given sometimes to the whole race and at other times to a particular people, Israel. These different dispensations are not separate ways of salvation. During each of them man is reconciled to God in only one way, i.e., by God's grace through the work of Christ that was accomplished on the cross and vindicated in His resurrection. Before the cross man was saved in prospect of Christ's atoning sacrifice, through believing the revelation thus far given him. Since the cross man has been saved by believing on the Lord Jesus Christ in whom revelation and redemption are consummated.

C. I. Scofield, ed. *The New Scofield Reference Bible* (New York, NY: Oxford University Press, 1969), 3 n. 3. See also John F. Walvoord, "Biblical Kingdoms Compared and Contrasted,'" in *Issues in Dispensationalism* (Chicago: Moody Press, 1994), 88.

on the day of Pentecost and is formed by the baptizing work of the Holy Spirit (Acts 2:1–2; 11:15–16; 1 Cor. 12:13).[29]

Scripture says, "it is required of stewards that one be found trustworthy" (1 Cor. 4:2). Therefore we are expected to fulfill our personal stewardship responsibility for God in a trustworthy and reliable manner. This duty extends to our management of material resources, talents and abilities, or time. It includes our relationship to others, and also entails our care for creation itself.

3. The Principle of Spiritual Growth: *God's Intention*

God is life and light (John 1:4). As light, God desires to reveal Himself to us. As life, God intends to produce spiritual growth in His people for His glory and has abundantly provided that opportunity for all Christians. But godly living with contentment can only be experienced as we continually engage in the pursuit of spiritual growth and maturity. 1 Peter 2:2 states, "like newborn babies, long for the pure milk of the word, so that you may grow in respect to salvation." We must recognize that the Christian's spiritual growth is a continual, life-long process. It is essential for continually developing and refining our maturity and discernment in the process of becoming until this earthly life is over.

4. The Principle of Distribution: *God's Distribution*

The fact of God's ownership also gives Him the right to dispense whatever He chooses in keeping with His sovereign

---

[29] See Chapter 8 in this book, which develops the Christian's relationship to the Holy Spirit in greater detail.

design and purpose. Scripture states, "But my God will supply all your needs according to His riches in glory in Christ Jesus" (Phil. 4:19). Many other things (e.g., people, circumstances, etc.) may be involved in the process, but God is ultimately responsible for distributing each individual's material resources, talents and abilities, and time. One of the most important areas of His distribution for every Christian is that of spiritual gifts and enablement—that which God provides to promote our spiritual growth and service.

5. The Principle of Balance: *God's Determination*

The study of God in Scripture, together with human history, clearly reveals the perfect balance of unity, diversity, and interdependence. This balance reveals God's sovereign design and purpose, and provides for the removal of conflict, confusion, and disharmony in the world. This balance is magnificently demonstrated in the harmony among the members of the trinity. In addition, God's balanced design for the body of Christ, with its many members all permanently indwelt and empowered by the Holy Spirit, provides great potential for Christ's church to declare the excellence of God to the world. "But now God has placed the members, each one of them, in the body, just as He desired" (1 Cor. 12:18).

6. The Principle of Spiritual Enablement: *God's Provision*

The Holy Spirit's permanent indwelling of every Christian, that began on the day of Pentecost, is the major distinctive of the church. It sets the body of Christ apart from any other body of believers in the past. The Christian's godly stewardship of material resources, talents and abilities, or time can only be accomplished by depending upon the Holy Spirit to do in us, for us, and through us, what we cannot do in our own strength. Paul writes, "But I say, walk by [in dependence upon] the Spirit and you will not carry out the desire of the flesh" (Gal. 5:16). Anything done apart from dependence on the Holy Spirit is the work of the flesh and cannot glorify God. One of the more familiar biblical subjects related to this dependence is the gifts of the Spirit—God given enablement for service. "But to each one is given the manifestation of the Spirit for the common good.... But now God has placed members, each one of them, in the body, just as He desired" (1 Cor. 12: 7, 13).

7. The Principle of Contentment: *Our Opportunity*

Contentment is the Christian's victory over covetousness. Covetousness occurs when a person desires what he does not have because he is dissatisfied with what he does have. Contentment is always available to the godly person who accepts whatever God provides as sufficient. Paul writes, "Not that I speak from want, for I have learned to be content in whatever circumstances I am" (Phil. 4:11). This person experiences contentment because he has not only learned that God's will is good, acceptable, and perfect, but he has also learned that the same God who promised to supply all of our needs can indeed be trusted, no matter what the circumstances. Hebrews 13:5 says, "Make sure your character is free from the love of money, being content with what you have, for He Himself has said, 'I will never desert you, nor will I ever forsake you.'" And Philippians 4:19 promises, "God will supply all your needs according His riches in glory in Christ Jesus."

CHAPTER 5

Stewardship of Material Resources: How to disburse what belongs to God (Part 1: 1 Timothy 6:1–19)

In this section we will be dealing extensively with two key passages of the New Testament Scriptures (1 Timothy 6:1–19, 2 Corinthians 8:1—9:15) that provide the essential guidance and instruction for the proper stewardship of material resources. Dr. Charles Ryrie comments on the importance of this subject when he states,

> One of the most important evidences of true spirituality is seldom discussed in books or sermons on the subject. We are prone to paint the image of spirituality in colors of deep Bible knowledge, lengthy times of prayer, or prominence in the Lord's work, which is not only deceiving but must be very discouraging to the average believer who can never envision these features as being part of his life. He concludes therefore, that these major manifestations of spirituality will never be seen in his life. To be sure, a vital spiritual life is related to fellowship with

the Lord in His Word and prayer and to service for the Lord and His work. But our love for God may be proved by something that is a major part of everyone's life, and that is our use of money. How we use money demonstrates the reality of our love for God. In some ways it proves our love for God more conclusively than the depth of knowledge, length of prayers, or prominence of service. These things can be feigned, but the use of our possessions shows us up for what we actually are.[30]

Before we delve into these two key passages, we need to consider how the Bible, as well as our current conditions, can throw some light on the urgent need to examine all of our stewardship responsibilities (material resources, talents and abilities, and time) while continuing to focus especially on our material resources.

When a Christian ignores or rejects God's truth or God's wisdom we resort to our natural fallen mind and man's wisdom. We determine that our explanations, plans or designs for dealing with the basic issues and questions of life are better, more sensible, workable or desirable than God's. The ultimate end of this exercise is filled with confusion, myths, fantasy, and lies that further remove us from the

---

[30] Charles C. Ryrie, *Balancing the Christian Life* (Chicago, IL: Moody Press, 1969), 87. We strongly recommend the entire chapter in this book entitled, "Money and the Love of God." It describes the proper stewardship of material resources, and does so in the clear, concise, and complete style so typical of Dr. Ryrie. It is significant to note that the book was first published nearly fifty years ago when the incredible affluence of the American society was really beginning to challenge and impact our Christian culture's stewardship of material resources with greater and more subtle intensity.

reality of God and eternal values. For example, in a recent *Time* magazine poll, a full sixty-one percent of Christians surveyed believe that God wants people to be prosperous, and thirty-one percent agreed that if you give your money to God, God will bless you with more money.[31]

Confusion, myths, fantasy, and lies abound. Realizing that this is not new, we must not overlook how easily God's people can be deceived, as well as the unsaved. A large portion of the Bible records the history of the nation of Israel, God's chosen people. Israel as a nation desired what it did not have because it was dissatisfied with what God's perfect plan and promises had graciously and bountifully provided (in violation of the principle of contentment). That is covetousness, and it infected every level of the nation from the kings (including Solomon, whom God blessed with unmatched wisdom, great power, and untold riches), to the priesthood, down to the common people. It led to all kinds of sins, including lust, greed, immorality, and idolatry, and finally culminated in the rejection and crucifixion of the Son of God, their promised Messiah.

The two thousand year history of the church clearly reveals that we have engaged in the same sins as the nation of Israel (lack of contentment and covetousness) regarding our stewardship of material resources. But, as the above survey indicates, the problem has been compounded by the growing biblical illiteracy among "born again" evangelical Christians who should understand or at least should have been taught that the New Testament never states or implies that God wants members of the body of Christ to be rich in

---

[31] David Wan Biema and Jeff Chu, "Does God Want You to be Rich?," in *Time* (September 10, 2006). Accessed at http://content.time.com/time/magazine.article/0,9171,1533448,00.html (June 4, 2015).

material resources. God's perfect plan for His Church reveals: "But my God will supply all your needs according to His riches in glory in Christ Jesus" (Phil. 4:19) and in our study of 1 Timothy 6:1–21, we will see how this sufficiently provides for Christians to experience *Godly living with contentment.*

As we begin to examine *how to manage God's material resources in response to God's perfect design and plan*, we would suggest that you begin by reading 1 Timothy 6:1–21, paying particular attention to the very specific instructions found in 6:6–19.

The focus of this passage is on godliness with contentment even while we are carrying out the stewardship of material resources in a trustworthy manner. Since we know that this particular stewardship is one of the most difficult for any of us to manage to the glory of God, it is no wonder that Paul describes doing it with contentment as "great gain" (6:6). To get the full impact of this we need to explain some of the things we see in the text.

The term "godliness" (6:6), or "godly life-style," includes the *pursuit* of such things as righteousness, godliness, faith, love, perseverance, and gentleness (6:11). This leads to the principle that: *Our total life commitment to God, His will, and engagement in the on-going transformation process is preliminary to our pursuit of godliness with contentment (Rom. 12:1–5; 1 Tim. 6:6, 11).* Success in that process is available because "we have all we need pertaining to life and godliness" (2 Pet. 1:1–11).

Notice that the word "gain" appears in both verses 5 and 6. In verse 5 it means the "provision" of money or other material possessions that a false teacher selfishly desires as he advocates doctrines that do not "...agree with sound words, those of our Lord Jesus Christ, and with the doctrines conforming to godliness" (6:3). The connection between teaching false doctrine and the desire for financial gain has always been one of the major characteristics of false teachers, and it abounds with fury in our society today. Paul points out that their practice causes "constant friction between men of corrupt mind, who have been robbed of the truth and who think that godliness is a means to financial gain" (6:5, NIV).

In contrast, Paul uses the word "gain" in verse 6 where he relates it to the "basic essentials" of food, clothing and shelter, as explained by the context of verses 6–8, where he says, "we brought nothing into the world, so we cannot take anything out of it either. If we have food and covering, with these we shall be content" (6:7–8). Another principle that is taught here is: *We came into the world with nothing and God promises to provide all the essentials for life (food, clothing and shelter, 1 Tim. 6:7–8; Phil. 4:19).* This is a vital outgrowth of our foundational principle of distribution and provides us with confidence in the principle: *As we learn that what He promises and provides is sufficient, we are content (1 Tim. 6:6–8).*

In spite of what false teachers do to obtain money or material resources from their corrupt efforts, or whatever those who are confused by the false teachers may suppose, godliness is *not* a means of financial or material gain (6:3–5). That's the old version of today's "prosperity theology" which teaches that the more you give, the more you get back. The Greek word for great is *megas*, where we get our modern day adjective "mega." That's super big, and it reinforces the positive and negative aspects of the principle we learn here: *Godliness is not a means of material gain, but godliness actually is a means of great gain when accompanied by contentment" (6:3–6).*

The word contentment in verse 6 means being sufficient and implies that God's provision alone is all that is needed to satisfy. It is an attitude of mind and heart, or a perspective of inner peace, that can only be learned as we let the indwelling Holy Spirit teach and enable us in our process of spiritual growth and maturing. As we combine the meaning of *contentment* with God's promised provision of basic essentials, Paul has taught us the principle: *Contentment is an attitude of mind and heart that has learned to be satisfied with God's provision as sufficient that is based upon trusting God and His promises (6:6–8).*

The same word for contentment is used in another passage that helps us understand its meaning. When Paul says,

> for I have learned to be content in whatever circums-
> tances I am. I know how to get along with humble
> means, and I also know how to live in prosperity;
> in any and every circumstance I have learned the
> secret of being filled and going hungry, both of having
> abundance and having need. (Phil. 4:11-12)

These verses teach us that (1) the learning process must not stop because we are subject to changes in the circumstances of our life, and (2) contentment is not permanent. But the good news is that we can experience contentment as long as we continue to learn and trust God for His provision based on His promises. An important key to our contentment is taught through Paul's own experience and formulated in the principle: *Even though contentment is not permanent because conditions and circumstances change, we can experience it as long we continue to learn and trust God to fulfill His promises (Phil. 4:11–12).*

Our attitude and practice regarding how we manage God's material resources, particularly money, is one of our most difficult areas of stewardship and most vividly demonstrates the reality of our love for God. Satan, the world system and the flesh intensify this struggle. They strive to convince us to pursue financial wealth above everything so that with it we can not only obtain other forms of material resources, but anything that may satisfy our selfish desires, such as popularity, power, pleasure, acceptance, and security. The challenge of being stewards of all that God has entrusted to us, even as we live in this affluent American culture, can only be effectively won by learning to be content with all that God provides according to His good, acceptable, and perfect will.

In verses 6-8, Paul has been explaining that God provides the *basic essentials* of life as the basis for our trustworthy stewardship as godly Christians. But in verse 9 he introduces a word that is especially important in regard to the stewardship of material resources. That is the word *"rich,"* and it appears again in verse 17. The context of 6:9–19 clearly shows us that in both instances the word is describing godly Christians who either want to have resources beyond the basic essentials, or have become responsible for material resources beyond the basic essentials where they must choose how they will use or manage them. We will be referring to resources beyond the basic essentials as "discretionary wealth." And verses 17–19 make it very apparent that most, if not all Christians currently living in our affluent American culture have far more than our basic essentials and therefore we are *rich.* Consequently,

Paul has identified the principle: *Godly Christians who are responsible for material resources beyond the basic essentials must choose how they will exercise trustworthy stewardship of their discretionary wealth ("riches," 1 Timothy 6:9–19).*

This portion of Scripture (6:6–19) teaches us that God is pleased when we experience godliness with contentment. We are to actively engage in pursuing godliness, while learning that God provides all that we need for life and godliness throughout our earthly existence regardless of the circumstances (2 Pet. 1:3). In addition, we see that God provides for most, if not all of us, additional *discretionary wealth.*

With all God is providing and over which we must be trustworthy stewards, are we struggling in the area of continually to learning to be content? If our answer to this question is yes, our failure to be content may be due to the fact that we have begun to desire what we do not have because we are dissatisfied with what we do have. In other words, we want to be *rich* because we are not content with God's provision for our *basic essentials* or we want more *riches* because we are discontent with God's provision of our *basic essentials* plus our *discretionary riches.* But before that happens and our contentment becomes covetousness, we must heed Paul's stern warning,

> But those who want to get rich fall into temptation and a snare and many foolish and harmful desires which plunge men into ruin and destruction. For the love of money is the root of evil, and some by longing for it have wandered away from the faith and pierced themselves with many griefs. (1 Tim. 6:9–10)

As a result, we need to immediately begin following the specific precepts that Paul identifies in 6:11–15.

Before we do that however, let's reflect upon the following spiritual considerations. First, since God owns everything (the principle of ownership), He has the right to dispense riches to one person and not to another (the principle of distribution).

Second, it is not wrong for godly Christians to have riches, or to have only the basic essentials and no riches, but in either case we are expected to exercise trustworthy stewardship of whatever basic essentials and riches God has provided (the principle of stewardship). At the same time, we are expected to keep learning (the principle of spiritual growth) to be content with God's present and future provision, since possible changes can take place in our circumstances (the principle of contentment). Such attitudes and behaviors can be experienced not only because everything belongs to God, but because His good, acceptable, and perfect will is interwoven with His perfect plan (the principle of ownership). With complete confidence, we can trust Him!

Now, let's return to verses 9–19. This passage can be divided into three parts. First, there is the warning that describes the danger of not being content with God's provision for our *basic essentials because* we want more *riches*. It is a disastrous pitfall, and the enemy relentlessly employs various schemes and devices to draw us into that trap (6:9-11). Second, the text details the marvelous response that God has provided—a solution that touches on every one of our foundational principles concerning how to deal with material resources with contentment (6:11–15). Third, Paul concludes with godly precepts and principles, together with timely applications designed to assist us in trustworthy stewardship of *discretionary wealth* (6:17–19). Now let's continue our exciting journey!

The context clearly shows us that the warning of 1 Timothy 6:9 is for godly Christians who find themselves in one of three stages: (1) experiencing contentment, or (2) desiring to experience contentment while engaged in the struggle, or (3) experiencing discontentment. Therefore the warning is directed toward every godly Christian as they demonstrate trustworthy stewardship of all the material resources, talent and abilities, or time that God is providing for them.

It is also helpful to notice the sharp contrast between contentment (6:6, 8), which we defined above as "an attitude of mind and heart or a perspective of inner peace...that can only be learned as we let the Holy Spirit teach and enable us in our spiritual growth and maturing process," and the strong language that is used in the warning. The word "want" (6:9) is a Greek word meaning to have a strong desire, or to be driven to want more. Some Bible scholars tell us that the word describes an obsession growing out of the reasoning of the mind. In observing these contrasting elements, we must look at the role of the "mind" as Paul says "do not be conformed to this world, but be transformed by the renewing of your mind, so that you may prove what the will of God is, that which is good and acceptable and perfect" (Rom. 12:2). We constantly face a struggle because the mind can be controlled by the old nature or controlled by the Holy Spirit who indwells and can transform our thinking process (Gal. 5:16).

As Paul contrasts the proper attitudes involved in contentment with the opposite attitudes found in the warning, he describes them as the drive or craving "...to get rich" (6:9) and "the love of money" (6:10). It has been correctly suggested that both of these are actually two sides of the same coin. Without question they vividly describe the quest and craving of humanity, especially in our affluent American society today. Verse 10 is not saying that money itself is the root of all evil, but rather the craving for money and greed exercised to acquire it is evil. In a parallel passage, the Apostle John says,

> Do not love the world nor the things that are in the world. If any loves the world, the love of the Father is not in him. For all that is in the world, the lust of the flesh and the lust of the eyes and the boastful pride of life, is not from the Father, but is from the world. (1 John 5:15–16)

In order to remove any question regarding source of all the ungodly desires revealed in the entire warning (6:9–10), note carefully what Ephesians 6:10–11 says, "so that you may be able to stand against the schemes of the devil. For our struggle is...against the rulers, against the powers, against the world forces of darkness, against the spiritual forces of wickedness..." (Eph 6:10–11).

As an illustration of the ever-present danger signified by the warning, Paul identified the church at Ephesus as a well-taught, growing, and mature body of believers that was excelling in all God intended for His Church and its members. They achieved this even though they lived in one of the most affluent and worldly cultures of their day, and even though they faced opposition and persecution. However, some thirty years later the Apostle John wrote God's message to the church of Ephesus, saying, "I know your deeds and your toil... and you have perseverance and have endured for My name's sake and have not grown weary. But I have this against you, that you have left your first love" (Rev. 2:2-4).

Remember what John said about those who love the world (1 John 2:16)? Clearly it was a love for the world and the things in the world learned from their culture that crippled the Ephesian church. Our current American culture has become at least as affluent and ungodly as the culture of Ephesus in the first century. Add to that the scientific and technological advances that provide incredible "things" we never imagined and now desire, together with a system of global satellite public and personal communications that bombard us constantly with messages designed to entice us into the world's philosophy and life-style. We are naïve to think we cannot be lured into their trap. From this we learn one thing for certain. No matter how long we walk close to God and no matter how long and faithfully we have served Him, it is still possible to stumble. The warning is clear—don't ignore it!

In summary, the contrast shows us that contentment, with all its marvelous benefits, can only be learned when we allow our mind to be controlled by the Spirit of God, producing the mind of Christ within us. At the same time, the contrast shows that the desire for and obsession with riches with its potential pitfalls and disastrous consequences can only increase their influence on our thoughts when we allow our minds to be controlled by the flesh, Satan, and the world. There is an old axiom that goes something like this, "our thoughts control our attitudes and our attitudes control our actions." The Bible lends credence to this when it says "For as a man thinks within himself, so he is" (Prov. 23:7).

If our thoughts determine our behavior then in reality our battle, such as our struggle between dissatisfaction and contentment, must first take place in our mind before it is expressed in our behavior. The struggles that are part of this process occur because when we were saved we became new creatures in Christ (2 Cor. 5:17) and the Holy Spirit came to live permanently within us to teach us God's Word and enable us to defeat the flesh and Satan. As a result our minds and hearts, which up to that point could only be controlled by our corrupt nature, received a new capacity to be controlled by the mind of God through the Spirit of God. The Bible describes this dual capacity with its competing terminology as (a) the old nature versus new nature, (b) flesh versus the Spirit, (c) the old man versus new man, and (d) carnal versus spiritual. Paul describes this struggle in Galatians 5:16–17,

> But I say, walk by the Spirit, and you will not carry out the desire of the flesh. For the flesh sets its desire against the Spirit, and the Spirit against the flesh; for these are in opposition to one another, so that you may not do the things that you please.

In our study of 1 Timothy 6:11–16, we now come upon some extremely helpful instructions that are built around three commands: "Flee from these things.... Fight the good fight of faith...keep the commandment without stain or reproach..." (6:11, 12, 14). These detailed precepts include both offensive and defensive strategies designed to enable godly Christians to effectively respond to the warning (6:10–11) and to engage in our stewardship of material resources, particularly as it relates to riches or discretionary wealth (6:17–19).

In the first command, "Flee from these things" (6:11), *these things* obviously refers to *the craving or greed for riches* (6:9) and *the love of money* (6:10), with an interesting addition to the command, "and pursue righteousness, godliness, faith, love, perseverance, and gentleness" (6:11) which are Spirit-enabled qualities that characterize the godly life-style. This command includes the two directives *flee* and *pursue,* and though they may appear contradictory, are actually complimentary. This two-part command is a call to employ the strategy that *the best defense is a good, strong offense.*

Our fleeing or escape from the ungodly craving or greed for riches and the love of money can only be suppressed or stopped when we refuse to let our minds and hearts be controlled by the flesh and let them be controlled by the Spirit of God as we pursue godly living with contentment (6:9, 11). In fact that pursuit enables us to develop those Spirit-enabled character qualities of a godly life-style that can only enhance our service of stewardship (6:11) which confirms the companion principle: *The best defense is a good, strong offense (6:9, 11).*

Furthermore, *pursuit* is a critical element in this concept of fleeing, because *pursuit* is a zealous, determined, and enthusiastic drive that is God's gracious means of escape from this temptation. This is the same strategy Paul taught the believers in Corinth when he said,

> No temptation has overtaken you but such as is common to man; and God is faithful, who will not allow you to be tempted beyond what you are able, but with the temptation will provide a way of escape also, so that you may be able to endure it. (1 Cor. 10:13)

Finally, this same *flight* and *pursuit* strategy is an effective defense against the attacks of our arch-enemy Satan. James 3:1—4:17 deals very practically with most of the issues we have been considering. But for our immediate focus, note the following quote from James 4:4–8:

> Therefore whoever wishes to be a friend of the world makes himself an enemy of God. Or do you think that the Scripture speaks to no purpose: He jealously desires the Spirit which He has made to dwell in us? But He gives a greater grace. Therefore it says, "God is opposed to the proud, but gives grace to the humble." Submit therefore to God. Resist the devil and he will flee from you. Draw near to God and He will draw near to you.

Did you catch it? When James says "resist the devil and he will flee from you" he uses the same word for *flee* that Paul used in 1 Timothy 6:11. It means *to get away from* or *escape*. Isn't it amazing and encouraging that when we resist Satan's control by our offensive pursuit of God, Satan is defeated and wants nothing to do with us?

As we turn to the second and third commands in this triad of precepts, we notice that the language and tone of the immediate context relate to warfare or military-type conflicts and final victory (6:12–16). This provides a realistic picture of the challenges and opportunities we face and the nature of our response. It also helps us make practical applications of the biblical truth. But before we examine these two commands more closely, it is important that we explain the inevitability of our involvement in this war, and provide the biblical background for all that is included in these verses (6:12–16).

Ever since Cain killed his brother Abel, biblical and secular history records the fact of countless wars, and today there are wars and rumors of war all over the world. But as members of the body of Christ, we find ourselves in the forefront of the greatest war—one that has been relentlessly waged by Satan and fallen man against God and His people ever since creation. Only physical death or the Rapture (when the church will be removed and taken to be with the Lord), will end our role as combatants in "fighting the good fight of faith" (6:11; see also 6:14–15; 1 Thess. 4:16–17). This war will continue until that battle which will ultimately end all wars when God, the supreme Commander in Chief, through His eternal Son, who has become the King of kings and Lord of Lords, will return to finally defeat, judge and destroy every enemy including Satan, every human being who has rejected God's gracious salvation, and even death. When that is accomplished, He will bring in His earthly, eternal kingdom with everlasting peace, over which His Son will reign. We will reign with Him because we are one with Him both now and forever.

In the meantime, we must "Fight the good fight of faith" (6:12). This command is addressed to the godly Christian who has obeyed the previous command to *pursue* (6:11). Consequently, we have a Christian, living a godly life-style, experiencing contentment, continuing to *pursue* godliness in order to maintain the growth and maturity necessary to more effectively exercise godly character qualities, who is now given the command to fight. As strange as it may seem for *fighting* to be described with the word *good* (6:12), which means right and honorable, when we realize who commands it and what it is designed to accomplish, it makes perfect sense, and we must obey. The word "fight" describes exerting strong effort in order to win a struggle. The fact that it is a present imperative emphasizes that we are not to quit, but to keep on fighting without letting up for one moment. All three action-packed commands are not addressed to spectators but participants because that's what we are! If the load appears heavy and the task impossible, it is. That's because they can only be accomplished when we depend upon the Holy Spirit doing in us, for us, and through us, what we cannot do in our own strength. Now belief and trust in that truth is the *faith* in the "fight of faith" (6:12). It is the same kind of faith that resulted in our eternal life when we believed that Jesus Christ, God's Son, died in our place for our sins and rose again (1 Cor. 15:1–11), and what Jesus explained when He said, "For God so loved the world that He gave His only begotten Son, that whosoever believes in Him should not perish but have everlasting life" (John 3:16).

In verse 12 Paul's command uses the word *fight* two times. From this Greek word (*agonizomai*) we derive our word agony, and metaphorically the word means to contend or strive perseveringly and relentlessly to win against opposition and temptation. Obviously, the fight is a very demanding struggle that requires reliance upon every bit of strength, ability, and energy that God provides.

Paul then attaches a supporting precept to the command to *fight* that reads, "take hold of the eternal life to which you were called, and you made the good confession in the presence of many witness" (6:12). Since this precept is written for Timothy to remind those mature, solidly grounded believers in Ephesus, Paul is not implying that they should become Christians by accepting Christ to receive eternal life. They are already saved, growing, and maturing. The Greek here is actually saying *get a grip on* or *get serious about* their eternal life. Therefore, when this precept instructing them, and us, *to flesh out* all of the meaning, substance, and value of their eternal life is combined with our good fight of faith against our formidable enemy (the world, the flesh and Satan) it defines a challenging encounter. Thus the principle: *As we are living a godly life-style, experiencing contentment, and continuing to pursue the godliness necessary to maintain maturity, we must also strive relentlessly to win against temptation by fleshing out all of the meaning, substance, and value of our eternal life by obeying God's precepts. (6:12).*

Therefore, the first thing we need to *get a grip on* is the fact that eternal life began the moment we were saved and to "fight the good fight of faith" is as much a part of the gift of eternal life as anything else in the growth and maturing process of the Christian life (that is, the pursuit of godly living and contentment). The second fact we need to get a grip on is wrapped up in the word "called," which means chosen, selected, or elected, and beautifully describes God's role in our salvation and our receiving eternal life. So Timothy is instructed to remind the Ephesians of the words in Paul's previous letter where he describes our salvation by saying that God before creating the world chose us in Himself and adopted us as sons through Christ to Himself according to His will (Eph. 1:3–4).[32]

---

[32] This is only part a very long sentence (Eph. 1:3–14) filled with such details of God's eternal purpose in calling us to eternal life that it staggers

The phrase, "And you made the good confession in the presence of many witnesses" (6:12) appears to be a needed reminder to Timothy, to the Ephesian believers, and to us of the principle: *Enriching our spiritual growth and maturity by obeying God's precepts is actually our good confession (6:12).* God uses that good confession as a witness to impact many people, both believers and unbelievers. In this context the phrase is telling us that whether it's fleeing or pursuing (6:10), fighting or taking hold of (6:11), we must apply this principle: *We need to keep on obeying God's precepts no matter what the circumstances, in order to maintain and strengthen our good confession before our fellow believers and the world for God's use and His glory (6:12).*

The presentation of the third and final precept in the group covers four verses (6:13–16) of our main passage (1 Tim. 6:6–19). This precept, like the first two, supports the need for obedience, yet it seems to focus even more strongly on the element of obedience because it is attached to a command that is broader in scope. This precept is designed to reinforce all of the instructions we've received in this major passage on the stewardship of material resources, while conveying a sense of urgency for us to intensify our on-going experience of godly living with contentment, our stewardship of material resources, and our process of becoming what God wants us to become.

The importance of this precept is apparent when Paul makes an appeal to the highest authority in the universe regarding our acceptance of and obedience to the command. He says "I charge you in the presence of God, who gives life to

_____

our finite minds. A careful review of the entire passage will give us a much better grip on eternal life and enhance fighting the *good fight of faith.*

all things, and of Christ, who testified that good confession before Pontius Pilate" (6:13). Perhaps we should pause and at least try to imagine the scene. We hear the words "keep the commandment without stain or reproach until the appearing of our Lord Jesus Christ, which will be at the proper time" (6:14–15) as we stand in the presence of God our Father, the Creator and giver of all life, and God the Son, our Savior who was crucified because of His good confession that He was God in the flesh and who is now the resurrected giver of eternal life to all who receive Him. In addition, we know that we are able to be a part of this awesome and humbling scene only because God the Holy Spirit is standing with us and in us, making us one with the Father and the Son. How can our response be anything short of falling on our face in praise and adoration to express our love and willingness to obey all that is commanded?

As we examine the precept, notice the emphasis on obedience in the word "keep." Our willingness to obey God's commands is one of the priority challenges in the pursuit of godly living. But the challenge is intensified by the words "without stain and reproach," which is a call to a moral purity that is essential in our daily living as we carry out our obedience (6:13). Finally, the words "until the appearing of our Lord Jesus Christ" (6:14) make it clear that we face this challenge until this earthly experience is ended by our physical death or the Rapture (1 Thess. 4:13–16). Without question, this precept presents over-whelming challenges that can only be effectively met by allowing the Spirit of God to control our minds and enable thoughts, attitudes and behavior in ways that glorify our gracious and merciful heavenly Father.

Now this precept plainly tells us that we are to keep "the commandment," but the precise identity of the commandment does not appear in the immediate text. That being the case, many competent Bible scholars arrive at the following conclusion, "The *commandment* is probably broader than any single law. It refers to the entire body of sound teaching Paul had been describing throughout this letter."[33] While we are not suggesting that such a conclusion is wrong or inappropriate, we strongly believe that when Paul added "until the appearing of our Lord Jesus Christ which He will bring about at the proper time" he had a specific precept in mind. In fact, we believe that in context the command is to *live by faith* (6:12). Additional support for this is found in Heb.10:32—11:1 where the biblical precept "the righteous man shall live by faith" (10:38) is also joined to the appearing of our Lord Jesus Christ.

Before we explain this entire passage, we need to get a grip on the precept "to keep the commandment." since it expresses God's intended desire for all believers that "the righteous will live by faith." (Hab. 2:4). Though it was given to the people of Israel by the Old Testament prophet Habakkuk, it is repeated three times by New Testament writers and thereby directed to every member of the body of Christ. Our discussion deals with these New Testament passages because they distinguish three different elements of that precept and guide us in its application the church.

The first use is Romans 1:16–17 where Paul places the emphasis and application of the precept on man's receiving *righteousness* through *believing the gospel.* He later describes

---

[33] A. Duane Litfin, "1 Timothy," in *The Bible Knowledge Commentary*, ed. John F. Walvoord and Roy B. Zuck (Wheaton, IL: Victor Books, 1983), 747.

the end product of that transaction for the believer with these words, "He [God the Father] made Him [God the Son], who knew no sin to be sin on our behalf, so that we might become *the righteousness of God* in Him" (2 Cor. 5:21, italics added).

The second passage is Galatians 3:11, where the precept clarifies the truth that a man can only be declared righteous (justified) in God's sight by *faith*, rather than by *works*. He later describes this application of this precept by saying, "For by grace you have been saved *through faith*; and that not of your-selves, it is the gift of God, *not of works*, so that no one may boast" (Eph: 2:8-9, italics added).

The third occurrence is in the book of Hebrews when the writer quotes the precept and says "The righteous man shall live by faith" (Heb. 10:38). This verse helps identify the commandment Paul refers to in 1 Tim. 6:14 because the context (Heb. 10:32–38) clearly shows that the writer is placing the emphasis on the Christian's life-style after salvation and the certainty of the appearance of Jesus. In other words, he is using the precept to teach us that the person who has been declared righteous by God through faith (Rom. 1:16–17) apart from works (Gal. 3:11), must now live by faith (Heb. 10:38). Hence, in both Hebrews 10:38 and 1 Timothy 6:14, living by faith is linked with the appearing of our Lord Jesus Christ.

As we further examine Hebrews 10:32–38, we observe that as the writer begins to tie this command requiring *present* obedience with the *future* appearing of our Lord Jesus Christ, he reminds his readers of their *past* experience as oppressed and persecuted believers (10:32–34). He knew that an effective way to fortify people for future trials was to remind them of the strength and courage they displayed while facing their previous trials. In reality, Hebrews 10:32–34 accurately serves as a profile of the Ephesian church. After surviving the same kind of ordeals, they had emerged with confident hope in Christ's return and greater confidence that God would provide sufficiently for every need as they excelled in all God intended for His church and its members even while living in one of the most affluent and ungodly cultures of their day.

It is apparent that few, if any of us, have experienced persecution and suffering close to that of the early church. However, we have pursued godly living with contentment while living in an affluent and increasingly ungodly culture, in which Satan constantly employs clever and deceptive schemes designed to oppose, distract, or draw us away from our confident hope and commitment to godly living with contentment, trustworthy stewardship, and our process of becoming what God wants us to become.

Hebrews 10:32–36 is commanding the church to remember God's sufficient provision through all our past ordeals, with the resulting confidence in God (10:32–34). It reminds us not to waver or throw away our confidence, which in itself is great reward (10:35). The ordeals are not over yet, and they may even become more intense. But no matter how difficult and long the conflict may be, we are to keep pursuing the will of God, knowing that the light at the end of the tunnel is actually the very thing we've been looking and waiting for— the appearing of our Lord Jesus Christ (10:36).

After encouraging and instructing us regarding the things that challenge our godly living with contentment, the writer ties our *present* and *future* together with some of the most magnificent and glorious words Christians have ever been told when he says, "For yet in a very little while, He who is coming will come, and will not delay. But My righteous one shall *live by faith*; and if He shrinks back, My soul has not pleasure in him" (Heb. 10:37–38, from Hab. 2:3–4). In order to fully appreciate and understand these words in conjunction with Paul's words in 1 Tim 6:14–15, we have written the following *paraphrase* of both passages. Here is what Habakkuk, Paul, and the writer of Hebrews are saying:

> In a very little while, or in a brief period of time according to God's time frame, while we continue to endure our ordeals, He who is coming will come right on schedule, at the precise time God has planned to bring it about and there will be no delay. But in the meantime, the righteous, we who are Christians, shall live by faith. In fact, there is no other way to please God.

As we return to 1 Timothy 6:6–19 and its command to walk by faith (6:13–15a), it is not difficult to understand that Paul would be prompted to lift up this inspiring expression of praise to the One he describes as "the blessed and only Sovereign, the King of kings and Lord of lords, who alone possesses immortality and dwells in unapproachable light, whom no man has seen or can see" (6:15b–16a).

When we seriously contemplate the greatness of our awesome God, together with our incredible privilege of knowing Him and His will, we really don't have any option but to obey His will, especially when Paul tells us *why we should obey* in the words, "To Him be honor and eternal dominion! Amen" (6:16b). In other words, Paul is telling us that when we live by faith, when we continue pursuing godly living with contentment, when we engage in trustworthy stewardship, or employ the process of becoming, the sovereign Ruler of the universe will receive the honor and glory He so abundantly deserves. Concisely stated, this leads to the principle: *When we live by faith, pursue godly living with contentment, and engage in the process of becoming, we are ready to function as trustworthy stewards whose use of our discretionary wealth abundantly glorifies God (6:13–19).* Now that's what it's really all about, and it's an amazing setting for Paul to teach us the precepts and principles of the stewardship of discretionary wealth that abundantly glorifies of God (6:17–19).

When we do this everything begins to fall in place, confirming the amazing principle: *God's sovereign rule in heaven works together with our obedience as His children here on earth to accomplish His will (6:13–19).* Then we can distinguish and appreciate the difference between the temporary and the permanent, between the things of heaven and the things of earth. This enables us to understand how we are citizens of the heavenly kingdom of God while being members of the human race on earth.

Allowing the Holy Spirit to fill our minds and hearts with the practical truth of this perspective will be very helpful as we turn to Paul's specific instructions concerning our management of the discretionary wealth God has entrusted to us (6:17–19). It will also be good to remind ourselves of the principle of ownership (God owns it all), the principle of stewardship (we are God's appointed servant stewards), and the principle of distribution (God alone determines the recipients and the amount of discretionary wealth).

Paul continues his instructions with two precepts conveyed in the words, "Instruct those who are rich in this present world not to be conceited or to fix their hope on the uncertainty of riches" (6:17a). These two precepts particularly highlight the challenge we face when we pursue godliness with contentment and live in an incredibly affluent American culture that continues to stray farther and farther away from God and His will for man. The core of the challenge stems from the reality that virtually all of us are *rich* and therefore must exercise trustworthy stewardship of discretionary wealth in this ungodly cultural context. Notice also that these precepts, like the warnings in verses 9-10, focus on thoughts and attitudes that represent acceptable desires for those caught up in the world system, but that can easily result in ungodly and destructive behavior for the Christian. The magnitude of this challenge that is intensified by the schemes and power of the enemy initially requires the awareness, acceptance and application of the precautionary principle: *To allow our mind and heart to be controlled by the world, the flesh and Satan leads to (1) the prideful belief that our riches are obtained by our ability and that (2) they are the source of our security (6:17a).* To combat that temptation we must jealously cling to the preventive principle: *Firmly committing our mind and heart to the control of the Spirit leads to confident trust in God alone as the ultimate hope and source for our security, as well as our basic necessities and discretionary wealth (6:17b).*

The first precept contains the word "*conceited.*" It comes from a Greek expression that means to be high-minded, and in this context is describing a person impressed with what *he* is convinced *he* has accomplished with *his* ability to obtain *his* wealth. The problem is *pride*, which we know comes from a mind controlled by the world, the flesh, and Satan, where resistance to God and His will flourishes. Remember that we have been given the solution to this problem—*flee* and *pursue* (6:11).

The second precept addresses a very serious, yet subtle issue because its perspective is not only accepted, but is even admired in our ungodly culture. It is avidly taught and advocated by those at the highest levels of the secular financial system. The concept is based on the belief that discretionary wealth is our source of security. Not only does Paul's precept tell the rich not to do this (6:17a), but the phrase "the uncertainty of riches" helps us understand something very important about riches. For when the wording of the original places the emphasis on the element of uncertainty, the verse is really saying "riches have wings" or "they can fly away." In other words, in spite of what our ungodly culture entices us to do, riches should never be regarded as our stability, hope, or security. Such uncertainty is easily understood by those who have experienced or know anything of America's economic Depression of the 1920's and 30's or the burst of the real estate bubbles in the 1980's and 90's, plus the current bankruptcies of financial institutions, corporations, cities, and nations.

The next phrase positively instructs the rich to fix their hope "on God, who richly supplies us with all things to enjoy" (6:17c). This provides an immediate way to correct ungodly thoughts by directing our thoughts and trust toward God. For He is the ultimate source for our security and is already richly supplying us with all things to enjoy, including our discretionary material wealth.

Unfortunately, the common application of the word "enjoy" in this verse by many godly Christians living in this affluent culture often goes something like this: whatever discretionary wealth is available after all of my necessary basic essentials are determined, God has said He has supplied some, if not all of it for me to enjoy. Depending upon the amount available, that might be a new or newer car, a new or larger house with more property, or a second home, a boat, an extended vacation, a cruise, and the list goes on and on.

A better approach, however, to obtain a balanced perspective on what God means by the word "enjoy" is to saturate our minds with the biblical truth behind our seven foundational principles, blended together with principles and precepts of godly living with contentment taught in 1 Timothy 6:6–19, and seasoned with the words of Jesus quoted by the Apostle Paul in his departing instructions to the Ephesian elders as he says:

> And now I commend you to God and to the word of His grace, which is able to build you up and to give you the inheritance among all those who are sanctified. I have coveted no one's silver or gold or clothes. You yourselves know that these hands ministered to my own needs and to the men who were with me. *In everything I showed you that by working hard in this manner you must help the weak and remember the words of the Lord Jesus, that He Himself said, "It is more blessed to give than to receive."* (Acts 20:32–35, italics added)

Then, as Paul continues we realize that this precisely lays out the basis for both our *enjoyment* and our stewardship responsibility stated in his words, "Instruct them to do good, to be rich in good works, to be generous and ready to share"

(6:18). Consequently, the words of Paul and Jesus (Acts 20:32–35) and the words of Paul's instructions (6:18) complement each other perfectly and confirm the principle: *Our greatest enjoyment to be derived from the discretionary wealth God has entrusted to us is in giving and sharing those material and spiritual resources by doing good, being rich in good works, and being ready to generously share (6:18; Acts 20:32–35).*

It is also refreshing to recognize how the positive directives (6:18) coincide with the three essential elements of *godly living with contentment* taught both here (6:6–19) and confirmed elsewhere in the New Testament. The identical Greek wording "to do good" (6:18) is found only one other place in Scripture. Paul uses it in Acts 14:17 to describe God's actions and it means to be like God and to do as God does. Is this not what godliness and the will of God is all about? We must know Him in order to know His will and to do it as we touch the lives of the saved and the unsaved. Listen to this clear teaching:

> Do not be deceived, God is not mocked, for whatever a man sows, this he will reap. For as one who sows to his own flesh will from the flesh reap corruption, but the one who sows to the Spirit will from the Spirit reap eternal life. Let us not lose heart *in doing good,* for in due time we will reap if we do not grow weary [we need patient endurance]. So then, while we have opportunity [it is urgent], let us do good to all people, and especially to those who are of the household of the faith." (Gal. 6:7–10, italics added)

As godly Christians committed to doing the will of God, we must apply this truth in exercising our stewardship of discretionary wealth.

1 Timothy 6:18 continues by saying that we are to be "be rich in good works." The word *rich* obviously means an abundant, enthusiastic attitude as modeled by God Himself, "who *richly* supplies us with all things to enjoy" (6:17b). The words "good works" together is better understood as an element of godly living when we read Paul's description of God's eternal purpose. He says "For we are His workmanship, created in Christ Jesus for *good works* which God prepared beforehand so that we would walk in them" (Eph. 2:10, italics added). Paul attaches our *good works* to (1) our gracious salvation provided by God the Father and the Son, (2) the purity of godly living He enables us to experience, and (3) the appearance of Christ.

> For the grace of God has appeared, bringing salvation to all men, instructing us to deny ungodliness and worldly desires and to live sensibly, righteously and godly in the present age, looking for the blessed hope and the appearing of the glory of our great God and Savior, Christ Jesus, who gave Himself for us to redeem us from every lawless deed, and to purify for Himself a people for His own possession, *zealous for good deeds*. (Titus 2:11–14, italics added)

What a marvelous and awesome privilege we have to be stewards of discretionary wealth.

The words "to be generous and ready to share, storing up for themselves the treasure of a good foundation for the future, so that they may take hold of that which is life indeed" (6:18–19) present our last directive for the stewardship of the discretionary wealth entrusted to us. The opening words *"be generous and ready to share"* describe action that is to begin immediately and continue on as riches are available. The Greek words and structure emphasize "being ready," and should be expressed, "be ready to distribute liberally; be ready to share." In the context of affluent America and the abundant discretionary wealth available for distribution and sharing by God's people, by his emphasis on readiness Paul is identifying the principle: *Trustworthy stewards must possess an attitude and desire to look for places and opportunities to distribute and share their discretionary wealth as the Holy Spirit provides direction, guidance, discernment and enablement (6:18–19).* This is how the body of Christ is designed to function as it is blessed by God's provision of discretionary wealth.

The end of this precept contains two phrases: (1) "storing up for themselves the treasure of a good foundation for the future, (2) so that they may take hold of that which is life indeed" (6:19). Earlier in this passage, Paul linked the command to *live by faith* in the present with the future appearing of our Lord Jesus Christ (6:14). The reality is that God-honoring attitudes and character qualities are displayed when we apply the principle: *It is absolutely necessary to constantly anticipate the imminent return of Christ to take us to be with Him in order to be able to experience godly living with contentment in the present (6:14; Jn. 14:1–3; Thess. 4:16–19; 1 Cor. 15:51–58; Titus 2:11–14; Heb. 10:37–39).*

When Paul indicates that by obeying the precepts we are "storing up for ourselves the treasure of a good foundation for the future" (6:19a), suddenly the ultimate objective of our stewardship of discretionary wealth is clearly revealed and accurately described as a "treasure." It is encouraging to know that Jesus used the word "foundation" when He said,

> Everyone who comes to Me and hears My words and acts on them, I will show you whom he is like, he is like a man building a house who dug deep and laid a *foundation* on the rock; and when a flood occurred, the torrent burst against that house and could not shake it, because it had been well built. But the one who has heard and has not acted accordingly is like a man who built a house on the ground without any *foundation*; and the torrent burst against it and immediately it collapsed and the ruin of that house was great. (Luke: 16:47–49, italics added)

How beautifully this description conveys the outworking of our principles of spiritual growth and contentment that, especially in the context (6:6–19), are so essential to godly life-styles and trustworthy stewardship of discretionary wealth.

We know that all "riches" are God's and not ours, and He has entrusted them to us to manage for Him by distributing and sharing them. But how gracious God is to bless us both now and in the future as defined in the principle: *Whatever God richly supplies for us to manage for Him, we are to give away now to accomplish His purposes while the process stores up for us treasures of a good foundation for the future (6:19a).* It becomes increasingly evident that the giving, distributing and sharing in our present earthly experience relates to the temporary and transient, the perishable, the earthly, corruptible and mortal things. But the receiving of our treasured reward and inheritance in our future heavenly life will relate to the permanent and eternal, the imperishable, the heavenly incorruptible and immortal things. Verses 18–19a precisely describe this principle Jesus declared with the words,

> Do not store up for yourselves treasures on earth, where moth and rust destroy, and where thieves break in and steal, but store up for yourselves treasures in heaven, where neither moth nor rust destroys, and where thieves do not break in or steal, for where your treasure is, there where your heart be also. (Matt. 6:19–21)

This represents the apex of all that's wrapped up in our Christian experience of godly living with contentment— impacting every aspect of our life-long stewardship of material resources, talents and abilities, or time. In fact, the unwavering belief and application of this principle by every Christian is the epitome of God's purpose and design for the body of Christ to both enrich the church and reach the world.

This principle was very meaningfully expressed in the journal of a young man during his training for work in missions around 1949 as he said "He is no fool who gives what he cannot keep to gain what he cannot lose." That man was Jim Elliot, who believed and lived that truth until 1956 when he and four other young missionaries gave their lives to reach the Auca Indians of Ecuador. One bible scholar who has quoted Elliot adds,

Paradoxically, it is in this giving away of the possessions that the world considers the key to the good life that a Christian may take hold of (cf. 1 Tim. 6:12) the good life that is truly life. The alluring but vain and plastic substitutes for life, supplied by an unhealthy attachment to material things, pale into worthlessness when compared with that life which is found in Jesus Christ.[34]

As we connect these magnificent facets with the final phase "so that we take hold of that which is life indeed" (6:19d), we see that these truths bring us full circle in exercising godly living with contentment as we carry out our stewardship of material wealth now, "so that we may take hold of or get a grip on that which is life indeed" (6:19d; cf. 6:12). In other words, to grasp, accept, and apply this principle *now* in our stewardship of material resources, as well as talents and abilities, or time, while we store up our *future* treasure is to get a grip on and *experience life indeed now!* Remember that our life in Christ is eternal and that eternal life began at the moment we were saved. God's desire has always been that every Christian experience "life indeed" during the earthly part of our eternal life. How beautifully that He demonstrates this by designing our privileged stewardship responsibilities to be both our blessed enjoyment now and our source of our future eternal benefits.

It is extremely difficult to avoid being negatively influenced by the current affluent and materialistic American culture and the world's political and economic system that dominates

---

[34] A. Duane Litfin, "1 Timothy," in *The Bible Knowledge Commentary*, ed. John F. Walvoord and Roy B. Zuck (Wheaton, IL: Victor Books, 1983), 748.

the society we live among. Though every American Christian struggles in this life-long earthly battle, we've learned that the philosophy behind it is not from God, but is designed and controlled by the world, the flesh, and the devil, and there is every indication that it will continue with increasing intensity. Fortunately, however, we have also learned that there is victory when we let the indwelling Holy Spirit's teaching of the Word, plus His power and enabling to prevent the flesh from controlling our thoughts, attitudes and behavior (Gal 5:16). The application of this truth provides those experiencing godly living with contentment the opportunity to share their living testimony and encourage their struggling brothers and sisters to experience life indeed!

Needless to say, there will never be any more demanding and spiritually discerning process for godly, affluent American Christians than the personal, one-on-one interaction with God needed to determine what represents our real basic essentials and what represents discretionary wealth. Our study of 1 Timothy 6 has been designed to assist all of us in that process. But we still have much to explore concerning God's abundant grace and privilege in this area of stewardship as we turn to our second key passage—2 Corinthians 8:1—9:15. Be assured that we will uncover many helpful principles and precepts for giving from God's perspective that can further assist us in this process and enrich our pursuit of godly living with contentment. Since we've already learned that godliness with contentment is available with God's provision of the basic essentials (1 Tim. 6:8), making this difficult determination must be a reachable objective.

Before we begin our exposition of 2 Corinthians 8:1—9:15, it will be an encouragement for us to examine 1 Corinthians

2:6–16. This passage is encouraging because it enables us to see exactly how Christians derive hope and fulfillment from that amazing principle declared by Jesus and Paul (Matt. 6:18–21; 1 Tim. 6:18–19a) when we read,

> ...but just as it is written, 'Things which eye has not seen and ear has not heard, and which have not entered into the heart of man, all this God has prepared for those who love Him,' for to us God has revealed them through the Spirit;...now we have received not the Spirit of the world, but the Spirit who is from God, so that we might know the things freely given to us by God. (1 Cor. 2:9–12)

This passage also informs us as to why the unsaved (natural) people who dominate and perpetuate the current ungodly American culture and its worldly economic and political system do not believe or ascribe to that principle. Note the words of 2:14, which state, "But the natural man does not accept the things of the Spirit of God, for they are foolishness to him; and he cannot understand them, because they are spiritually appraised." See how blessed we are to have the Spirit of God that enables us to understand the wisdom of God, "which none of the rulers of this age has understood; for if they had understood it they would not have crucified the Lord of glory" (2:8). As pathetically sad as this picture is, we must never forget that we too were in the same condition as the Ephesian Christians, whom Paul earlier described with these words,

> And you were dead in your trespasses and sins, in which you formerly walked according to the prince of

the power of the air, of the spirit that is now working in the sons of disobedience. Among them we too all formerly lived in the lusts of the flesh, indulging the desires of the flesh and of the mind, and were by nature children of wrath, even as the rest. (Eph. 2:1–3).

These were the same people who were being instructed by Timothy to pursue godly living with contentment and ultimately apply the principle to the point of experiencing life indeed!

Finally, this passage and the related transformational truth challenges us to respond to the special evangelistic opportunity available to us in the midst of these unusually dark times, for you know that light shines brighter in darkness. Unquestionably, the heart of God would be pleased to use our shining testimony of godly living with contentment expressed in life indeed to bring some of the unsaved, with whom we daily rub shoulders, to accept Jesus Christ as Savior.

Summary Principles from 1 Timothy 6:6–19

Our total life commitment to God, His will, and engagement in the on-going transformation process is preliminary to our pursuit of godliness with contentment (Rom. 12:1–5; 1 Tim. 6:6, 11, p. 48).

We came into the world with nothing and God promises to provide for us all the essentials for life (food, clothing and shelter). As we learn that what He promises and provides is sufficient, we are content (1 Tim. 6:6–8, p. 49).

Contentment is an attitude of mind and heart that has learned to be satisfied with God's provision as sufficient that is based upon trusting God and His promises (1 Tim. 6:6–8, p. 50).

Godly Christians who are responsible for material resources beyond the basic essentials must choose how they will exercise trustworthy stewardship of their discretionary wealth ("riches," 1 Timothy 6:9–19, p. 52).

The best defense is a good strong offense; we must also strive relentlessly to win against temptation by fleshing out all of the meaning, substance, and value of our eternal life by obeying God's precepts (1 Tim. 6:9, 12, pp. 58, 62).

When we live by faith, pursue godly living with contentment, and obey God's will, we become trustworthy stewards whose use of our discretionary wealth abundantly glorifies God (1 Tim. 6:13–19, p. 69).

God's sovereign rule in heaven works together with our obedience as His children here on earth to accomplish His will (1 Tim. 6:13–19, p. 69).

To allow our mind and heart to be controlled by the world, the flesh and Satan leads to (1) the prideful belief that our riches are obtained by our ability and that (2) they are the source of our security (1 Tim. 6:17a, p. 70).

Firmly committing our mind and heart to the control of the Spirit leads to confident trust in God alone as the ultimate hope and source for our security, as well as our basic necessities and discretionary wealth (1 Tim. 6:17b, p. 70).

Trustworthy stewards must possess an attitude and desire to look for places and opportunities to distribute and share their discretionary wealth as the Holy Spirit provides direction, guidance, discernment and enablement (1 Tim. 6:18–19, p. 75).

It is absolutely necessary to constantly anticipate the imminent return of Christ to take us to be with Him in order to be able to experience godly living with contentment in the present (1 Tim. 6:14; cf. Jn. 14:1–3; Thess. 4:16–19; 1 Cor. 15:51–58; Titus 2:11–14; Heb. 10:37–39, p. 75).

Whatever God richly supplies for us to manage for Him, we are to give away now to accomplish His purposes while the process stores up for us treasures of a good foundation for the future (1 Tim. 6:19, p. 76).

CHAPTER 6

Stewardship of Material Resources: How to disburse what belongs to God (Part 2: 2 Corinthians 8:1—9:15; 1 Corinthians 16:1-4)

2 Corinthians 8:1—9:15 is the second major New Testament passage in our study dealing with the stewardship of material resources. This passage is helpful first, because it clearly explains sound biblical principles, precepts, and guidelines essential for carrying out the gracious ministry of Christian giving God has entrusted to us as stewards. Second, these two chapters describe events and decisions that demonstrate what happens when the body of Christ properly submits to the direction and enablement of the Holy Spirit in grace giving. This is one of the most significant and meaningful ways the church fulfills God's intended purpose in ministering to one another—by loving, giving, and sharing for the glory of God and for the common good (1 Cor. 12:7).

A number of conditions and circumstances surrounded the Corinthian Christians of Paul's day that are incredibly similar to those we face as twenty-first century American Christians. Our description of these parallel conditions can help us recognize how the truth in these two chapters is extremely relevant for us today.

For example, the Corinthians were subjected to an educated culture that exalted man's wisdom over God's. Consequently numerous strange concepts and philosophical ideas developed to explain man's existence and purpose. The culture also believed that the preaching of the cross was foolishness (1 Cor. 2:6–16). Such an environment vividly parallels our sophisticated culture where agnostic, atheistic and pseudo-intellectual concepts dominate. Evolution is taught in American educational institutions as truth, false world religions and atheism are increasing, while any expression of Christianity and belief in Christ as the way, the truth, and the life is belittled and violently opposed.

The Corinthians were also subjected to an affluent culture dominated by powerful political and commercial systems controlled by the world, the flesh and Satan. These systems perpetuated wicked, pagan philosophies and cultivated an extremely immoral, lustful, wicked, and ungodly population just like the one that surrounds us. Certainly these negative parallels are increasingly obvious and challenging.

But we can thank God for an important positive similarity that makes this relevant truth so practically appropriate for our application. A review of Paul's second missionary journey in the book of Acts, plus a careful examination of his first letter to the Corinthians, reveals that the congregation at Corinth had received as much, if not more sound teaching and written instruction than most of the early churches. Unlike the experience of most churches that grew out of Paul's mission efforts, God uniquely provided eighteen months of concentrated and uninterrupted foundational teaching through Paul and his co-workers as the church was being planted (Acts 18:1–17). During the next five years, as follow-up to intervening contacts and communications the Corinthians received Paul's two letters which contained commendation, correction, clarification and confirmation of all the truth they had been previously taught.

The parallel is obvious. They had received all the truth they needed to understand the foundational principles we've identified. They understood the necessity for every member of the body of Christ to submit to God and His will, and pursue godly living with contentment to the point of trustworthy stewardship of all God had entrusted to them and to employ the process of becoming. We also have received that truth—and more. In fact, we have multiple reliable translations and copies of the entire Bible, including all of the New Testament with their detailed instructions for us as members of the body of Christ during this earthly life and with Christ forever. Today, we also have access to material and opportunities that can provide the finest Bible study and training, often at little or no cost.

The context of Paul's second letter, particularly chapters 8:1—9:15, indicates that many had positively responded to the truth that they had already received. They were ready to digest and appropriately apply these additional instructions to enhance their on-going ministry of Christian giving. As American Christians our parallel opportunity and challenge is before us, so let's begin our examination of this passage.

As Paul begins his instructions to the Corinthian church in chapter 8:1–24, he points to the example of giving by the Macedonian churches in Philippi, Thessalonica, and Berea (8:1). He tells how they gave to support the saints in Jerusalem who were actually located over seven hundred miles away (8:4). Until these first four Gentile European churches were being planted, they didn't know that twenty-five years earlier the nation of Israel had rejected her Messiah. They did not realize that in concert with the Roman empire, they crucified Christ, making the unbelieving nation of Israel the conduit through which God brought salvation to both the Gentles and the Jews. Nor did they understand that when God raised Christ from the dead and sent His Holy Spirit to begin the Church in Jerusalem on the day of Pentecost, it was that same godless empire and the unbelieving rulers of the nation of Israel that orchestrated opposition against the six thousand plus membership of the newly formed Jerusalem church to the point of social devastation, poverty, and death. And they certainly were not aware that one of the principal leaders of that persecution was Saul (Acts 8:1–3) who was later called Paul (Acts 13:9), whom God said "he is a chosen instrument of Mine, to bear My name before the Gentiles and kings and the sons of Israel" (Acts 9:15).

So as Paul planted these Gentile churches, he obviously explained how his presence in Europe and their acceptance of Christ was evidence of their spiritual heritage that grew out of the evangelistic enthusiasm of the Jerusalem church and their subsequent suffering for Christ in the spread of the gospel. The context of our key passage (2 Cor. 8:1–24) clearly indicates that he had informed them of the material needs of these Jerusalem saints resulting from the affliction in which he had played key role.

There is one more important background element. That is the fact that, unlike the affluent and more protected environment of the Corinthian church in Greece, the churches in Macedonia, nearly two hundred miles to the north, were suffering much like the Jerusalem saints at the hands of unbelieving Jews and the ungodly Roman government resulting in a condition of poverty. For in addition to social and religious persecution, the Roman government had taken possession of all Macedonian silver and gold mines, heavily taxed the copper and iron smelting, and canceled their right to cut trees for ship and home building, all of which added to their severe poverty.

With all of this information, Paul begins to address the Corinthians with these words, "Now brethren, we wish to make known to you the grace of God which has been given to the churches of Macedonia" (8:1). By using the phrase "the grace of God" Paul immediately makes grace the centerpiece of the experience of these churches. Grace is a difficult concept to fully comprehend, but as we learned from our salvation experience, grace is received by everyone who accepts Christ as Savior. In recognizing that reality, grace begins to make sense and our salvation experience actually gives us an accurate and workable definition of grace as unmerited favor because (1) we didn't deserve it, and (2) it can never be earned.

At the moment we were saved, in grace the Holy Spirit took up permanent residence in us (1 Cor. 2:12; 6:19), bringing a new, divine nature and the enablement to know and do God's will as a minister of His grace in showing and sharing that grace to others.

That's the grace-giving concept Paul is talking about in 2 Cor. 8:1 as he continues his description:

> that in a great ordeal of affliction their abundance of joy and their deep poverty overflowed in the wealth

of their liberality. For I testify that according to their ability, and beyond their ability, they gave of their own accord, begging us with much urging for the favor of participation in the support of the saints, and this, not as we had expected, but they first gave themselves to the Lord and to us by the will of God. (8:2–5)

Notice first of all the closing phrase, "but they gave themselves *first* to the Lord and *then* to us *in keeping with God's will"* (8:5b, NIV, italics added). What we have repeatedly discussed bears repeating since this phrase states the essence of godly living with contentment. *Dissatisfaction, disobedience and the difficulties that accompany the desire for godly living with contentment will distort the experience of even well-intentioned Christians until we recognize that if we are going to know and do the will of God we must first give ourselves to God.*[35]

A magnificent display of the will of God that dramatically impacted every aspect of the Macedonian congregations was their ministry of grace giving. But there is another very important evidence of the Holy Spirit's working in and through these congregations that Paul points out when he says, "they gave of their own accord" (8:3). Both the language used in this phrase plus the issues mentioned in the surrounding context—such as great ordeal of their affliction, their abundance of joy, their deep poverty, their wealth of liberality (8:2), and their

---

[35] Paul explains this more effectively and completely than we ever could with the words "Therefore, I urge you, brothers, in view of God's mercy to offer your bodies as living sacrifices, holy and pleasing to God – this is your spiritual act of worship. Do not conform any longer to the pattern of this world, but be transformed by the renewing of your mind. Then you will be able to test and approve what God's will is – His good, pleasing and perfect will." (Rom. 12:1-2 NIV)

begging for the favor of participation (8:4), tell us that when these believers were informed of the plight and the needs of their fellow Jerusalem saints, the Holy Spirit prompted their voluntary and willing response without any other pressure or persuasion. Paul uses the Macedonian example to effectively show us how vital the Holy Spirit's role is in our personal and corporate ministry of grace giving to initiate and direct our stewardship of material resources.

No matter how strong and encouraging our biblical beliefs about grace giving might be, some questions and concerns might arise when we reflect on the manner in which giving is handled in most of our sound Bible-teaching churches and organizations. Over sixty years ago a very capable and respected Bible scholar and teacher said in an article entitled "Spirit Directed Giving:"

> Two widely separated methods of giving and of securing gifts are abroad in the Christian world. The one most commonly employed in churches and Christian gatherings is that of a direct appeal, often going so far as to suggest to the giver the amount they should give. The other method is that of depending only on the Spirit of God to direct the gifts in the case of every person, and then be willing to abide by the results of this confidence and trust.[36]

The article then clarifies the difference between *information* and *solicitation*, while stressing the importance of accurate, reliable information. The title given to this

---

[36] Lewis Sperry Chafer, *Spirit-Directed Giving* (Dallas, TX: The Central American Mission, n.d.), 1.

approach by the author is *information without solicitation* and it accurately describes the Macedonian experience. Later in the article he said,

> there is a difference between being told by God and being told by men as to what and where we should give; and the giver who is so dull of soul that he gives only under human pressure and responds only to strong emotional appeals will know nothing of the true grace of giving. [37]

Is it possible that the increasingly affluent and materialistic American culture of the last fifty to sixty years has influenced us to the point of substituting God's instructions for grace giving with adaptations of worldly techniques and strategies used for development programs, promotional advertising, fund raising, and the campaigns of non-profit secular institutions and charities?

Just as the Holy Spirit was the core player in the Macedonian's decision to give (8:3–5), the manner in which they responded (8:2–3) was so incredibly unusual that it cannot be explained apart from the supernatural work of the Holy Spirit. Expressed in a guiding principle: *The Spirit's control enables us to resist the influence of the world, the flesh and Satan in the decision making process and the Spirit's power enables us to engage in godly behavior and miraculously perform beyond our natural ability (8:2–5).* When those kinds of things take place, the world is confounded, worldly believers are mystified and Spirit-controlled believers praise and glorify

---

[37] *Ibid.*

God because it's not natural. For if in severe trials Christians experience overflowing joy (8:2b) and when poverty-stricken Christians express rich liberality (8:2b), that sort of human behavioral response can only be explained as the supernatural work of our God.

Paul says to the Corinthians and to us, "For I testify that according to their ability and beyond their ability, they gave out of their own accord, begging us with much urging for the favor of participation in the support of the saints" (8:3-4). Paul essentially closes his description of the Macedonian example by again reminding us that when we submit to the power and control of the Holy Spirit, then God can do in us and through us what we cannot accomplish in our own strength. But before we leave this example we need to take note of two additional principles of giving carefully woven through this report (8:1-5).

It has usually been the tendency to focus on wealthy Christians when giving is discussed. But ironically God selected the poverty-stricken Macedonians and their spectacular giving experience to teach the Corinthians and us a universal principle: *God has granted the privilege and responsibility of giving to every believer whether wealthy or poor (8:2-5).* Jesus also gave credence to this principle with the illustration of the poor widow by saying "...she, out of her poverty, put in all she owned, all she had to live on" (Mark 12:44; Luke 21:3-4).

The words of Paul's testimony, "that they gave as much as they were able, and even beyond their ability" (8:3, NIV) not only imply the Holy Spirit's involvement in their supernatural accomplishment, but they also indicate that another principle was in play. That is the principle: *the assurance of God's promised supply (Phil. 4:19) instills total confidence for Spirit-directed giving, since we know that God will meet every material need we have regardless of any circumstances created by obeying His will (8:3).* This principle instills in us total confidence for Spirit-directed giving, knowing that God will meet every material need we have regardless of any circumstances created in obeying His will. It also implies our recognition of the importance of giving ourselves first to the Lord in experiencing the Spirit's control (8:5b). All of these elements working in concert made it possible for the Macedonians to provide us with such a practical model for our ministry of grace giving.

In summary, it seems appropriate to note that in just five brief verses (2 Cor. 8:1–5), God has provided us with His ideal picture for both individual stewardship and the corporate handling of material resources. It touches on every essential issue related to godly living with contentment in the body of Christ and in the world. God sovereignly used the Macedonian church to inspire and set the Corinthians on course. But as Paul concludes the Macedonian story, we will learn that the Corinthians' performance, though commendable for the presence of many spiritual character qualities (8:7), did not measure up to the Macedonian model of gracious giving. The adjustment needed to prove the sincerity of their loving commitment (8:8) should be especially helpful for us, since the spiritual background and intellectual, ungodly, and affluent culture of the Corinthians is so similar to ours.

In verse 6, it is evident that having inspired them through the Macedonian account, Paul felt the need to dispatch Titus to Corinth to complete administering the collection from the four European churches for the saints of Jerusalem (cf.

8:16–24) and to help the Corinthian church complete the collection they enthusiastically began a year earlier (8:6). In fact, Paul commends them for being the first church that desired to give, as well as beginning to do it (8:10), but for some reason this *gracious work* (8:6) had not been completed.

Paul then commends the Corinthians for exercising spiritual gifts with abounding godly character in these words, "But just as you abound in everything, in faith and utterance and knowledge and in all earnestness and in the love we inspired in you" (8:7a). However, when he adds, "see that you *abound* in this gracious work as well" (8:7b), Paul is telling them that grace is the one character quality that needs to increase in order to reach the level of abounding. By using the Greek expression translated "gracious work" (8:6, 7), Paul is actually explaining that "giving is the essence of grace," which means that grace and giving are one and the same. Therefore, our guiding principle is *to abound in giving is to abound in grace and to abound in grace is to abound in giving (8:6, 7).*

When Paul adds "I am not speaking this as a command, but as proving through the earnestness of others the sincerity of your love also" (8:8), he is telling them that his previous statement is not intended as a motivating command, because he was confident that their original action was not the response to an external command. Instead, Paul knew that their concern for the Jerusalem saints was an expression of the love of God that had been poured out in their hearts and activated by the indwelling Holy Spirit. Furthermore, he was convinced that in light of all that had been accomplished in Macedonia and Corinth as a result of the Spirit's original call to action, the Corinthians would move forward as they responded to the same internal direction by the Spirit in desiring to prove the sincerity of their love through the completion of their grace giving.

By abounding in this gracious work (8:7), the Corinthians would display the normal pattern of God's love and grace working together. Consider the display of the abounding love of God the Son for us as proven in Paul's words, "For you know the grace of our Lord Jesus Christ, that though He was rich, yet for your sakes became poor, so that you through His poverty might become rich" (8:10). Now, by considering how the abounding love of God the Macedonians had for the Jerusalem saints was proved by their exemplary giving (8:1–5), we can understand his goal for the Corinthians in proving the sincerity of their love also (8:7).

Assuming that the Corinthians would positively respond to his encouraging suggestions and counsel, Paul begins to address relevant issues that needed both their consideration and action in order to properly progress toward the goal. As we carefully read the next three verses (8:10–12) we recognize that there are three basic elements of grace giving; (1) desire to do it, (2) begin to do it, and (3) finish doing it. The word "readiness" means eagerness or willingness, and refers to the Spirit-prompted readiness the Corinthians had demonstrated in their desire to give and their beginning to give, but they needed to finish their giving. In so doing Paul defines the principle of *Spirit-directed giving that includes readiness in regard to all three of these elements, implies that God's sufficient enablement and provision will empower all three (8:10–12).*

The follow-up statement "But if the readiness is present, it is acceptable according to what a person has, not according to what he does not have" (8:12), provides the assurance that we can trust God for two very important things. The first is that when the Spirit initiates the desire, that is when the available resource can be identified. Our omniscient God has already made the calculation according to His sovereign design and plan. Consequently, there is no need for hesitation or delay. The second is that God's calculation is based upon our confidence that He never asks us to give or administer anything that He has not already given to us. To put it plainly and simply, *it is our trust in God that enables us to give when the Spirit directs in keeping with what God has already provided (8:10–12).*

Paul continues to build confidence in grace giving by drawing attention to the principle of balance that is so essential to enabling the body of Christ to function with "equality" for every member (8:13–14). The word *equality* means *fairness,* about which we hear so much today in our ungodly affluent culture. Our examination of verses 13–15 explains how *fair* treatment is accomplished in the body of Christ and how our grace giving is employed by the Spirit of God to accomplish that fair treatment.

We can be confident that conditions of both need and grace-giving are not allowed by God for the purpose of creating ease for some and affliction for others (8:13). To the contrary, *God graciously uses them both to achieve equality through the effective functioning of the body of* Christ *(8:13–14).* So when Paul adds "at this present time your abundance, being a supply for their need, so that their abundance also may become a supply for your need, that there may be equality" (8:14), it is obvious that the "mutual compassion, concern and care" for one another is at the heart of his explanation. This is what Paul had explained to the Corinthians earlier about the functioning of diverse members of the living body of Christ (1 Cor. 12:23–26). In that explanation he used the divinely created human body as the illustration of the body of Christ and summarized this particular point of his instruction by saying "But God has so composed the body, giving more abundant honor to the member which lacked, so that there may be no division in the body, but that the members may have the same care one for another" (12:24b–25).

Paul's quote from Exodus 16:16–18 (8:15) confirms that the divine pattern for this principle was modeled about fifteen hundred years earlier when God gave food to the Israelites in the wilderness and He did so equally according to their needs. As the principle of balance results in equality or fair treatment, God does not always employ the same methodology to accomplish it. In the case of the Israelites, God totally controlled the supply and method of distribution.

Beginning in verse 16 and continuing through chapter 9:15, Paul develops two related areas for our benefit. First, he continues to show us more about how privileged we are as Spirit-enabled co-laborers with Christ to have the opportunity of ministering to the needs of one another in the body of Christ through grace giving. Second, Paul unfolds truths that enable us to zero in on helpful biblical principles that need to be applied as we engage in Spirit directed grace giving. Those principles will be clearly stated as the passage is presented and explained.

Paul had dispatched Titus (8:6) to revitalize his previous ministry to the Corinthians and assist them in completing their offering. As he reintroduces that plan, he describes Titus and his response to the request with these refreshing words: "But thanks be to God who puts the same earnestness on your behalf in the heart of Titus. For he not only accepted our appeal, but being himself very earnest, he has gone to you of his own accord" (8:16–17). The word "earnestness" means "zealous care or concern" for those we are called upon to serve. Members of the body of Christ are to minister to one another, particularly those in need. Notice also that this character quality is placed in our hearts by God, even as He did in Titus (8:16). By combining these elements with Paul's indication that the Corinthians abounded in "all earnestness" (8:7), we can clearly see how their original, zealous compassion and concern for the Jerusalem saints stimulated their willingness to gather an offering and inspired the Macedonians to do the same.

In addition we discover that Paul appointed two qualified "brothers" to travel with Titus to gather the offerings from the Macedonian churches and assist the Corinthians complete their collection. Paul describes the team by saying,

> We have sent along with him the brother whose fame in the things of the gospel has spread through all the churches; and not only this, but he has also been appointed by the churches to travel with us in this gracious work, which is being administered by us for the glory of the Lord Himself, and to show our readiness,... We have sent with them our brother, whom we have often tested and found diligent in many things, but even more diligent, because of his great confidence in you. As for Titus, he is my partner and fellow worker among you; as for our brethren, they are messengers of the churches, a glory to Christ. (8:18–19, 22, 23)

Take note of the list of credentials: earnestness (8:16); very earnest (8:17); appointed by the churches (8:19); often tested and found diligent (8:22); a partner and fellow worker (8:23) and a glory to Christ (8:23).

Paul appointed this team with their particular assignment, describing each member's effective ministry background along with their spiritual and moral integrity. From this we derive the principle that *only godly people with spiritual maturity and tested ministry experience should handle financial matters (8:18–19, 22, 23).* Every effort to accept and apply this principle should be made by churches today on the part of both those who give and those who administer such "gracious works for the glory of the Lord Himself" (8:19b).

In discussing who should administer, Paul also tells us how this *gracious work* should be administered by injecting "and to show our readiness, taking precaution that no one will discredit us in our administration of this generous gift, for we have regard for what is honorable, not only in the sight of the Lord, but also in the sight of men" (8:19b–20). This statement clearly supports the principle that *the financial matters of these gracious works should be administered honestly, expediently, orderly and openly (8:19–20),* in order to fulfill in timely fashion, our accountability to God, the body of Christ, and before the world, thus displaying God with the glory that belongs to Him.

Having concluded his instructions regarding the administration of this gracious work, Paul again challenges the Corinthians to complete their offering by saying, "Therefore openly before the churches, show them the proof of your love and of our reason for boasting about you" (8:24). Since Paul previously indicated that he was not *commanding* them to finish (8:9), he is now laying the groundwork for a principle that needs to be applied. Good beginnings are commendable, and we know that Paul has repeatedly boasted about theirs, even as he does again by saying "It is superfluous for me to write to you about this ministry to the saints, for I know your readiness, of which I boast about you to the Macedonians, namely that Achaia has been prepared since last year, and your zeal has stirred up most of them" (9:1–2). Unfortunately good beginnings like good intentions require fulfillment, especially in response to Spirit directed tasks assigned to members of the body of Christ pursuing godly living with contentment. God not only expects tasks to be completed, but He promises all the enablement and provision needed for that completion. In other words, the principle that Paul's exhortation supports is: *God provides all that is needed for the expedient beginning and completion of every Spirit directed task (9:1–2)*. In that way, God's good, acceptable and perfect will is accomplished, bringing glory to Himself and great blessing to believers and non-believers. God the Father and God the Son both model this principle by fulfilling every promise they make, and we properly imitate the Lord when we complete our gracious work.[38]

---

[38] With our attention drawn to God's provisions for beginning and completing Spirit directed tasks, it seems appropriate to encourage you to evaluate your application of this principle in completing the reading of the book. Assuming that your study with us to this point is your response to a Spirit directed task in the will of God, you like the Corinthians are to be commended for your excellent beginning. Since we firmly believe the Spirit directed us to write this book in obedience to the will of God, we have applied the principle in beginning and completing the task with the sincere desire to fulfill the objective described in the beginning of the book. We deeply hope that you finish the journey with us because, as you have already learned, our intention has been to completely, accurately

At this point, we must interrupt our discussion of chapter nine and examine the brief companion passage (1 Cor. 16:1–4) in the letter Paul had written to the Corinthians months earlier. It is necessary to do this so that our study includes all of the instructions Paul gives them regarding the offering for the Jerusalem saints and regular grace giving. After mentioning the topic of the offering (16:1) he lays down three principles that apply to such special offerings, as well as our regular giving when he says: "On the first day of the every week each one of you is to put aside and save, as he may prosper, so that no collection be made when I come" (16:2).

This verse provides the basis for the first principle: *Our giving should be handled regularly and thoroughly (1 Cor. 16:1–2).* This personal and private action should be carried out by each person every Sunday on a regular, weekly basis. The action described in this verse implies a process that requires time for a thorough, prayerful, and Spirit-directed assessment to determine our current material resources that are available for giving. This is apart from those needed for the on-going expenses of our basic necessities. Once those discretionary funds for giving are identified, they are to be put safely aside for that purpose only, awaiting the Spirit to direct our disbursement in grace giving.

With all of the confusing and conflicting traditions that have been taught and practiced over the recent centuries by the Church regarding the manner in which the first day of

---

and concisely describe how *godly living with contentment* through *trustworthy stewardship of our material resources, talents and abilities, or time* is available to every Christian in keeping with the clear teaching of the Scriptures.

the week (Sunday) is to be observed, it may surprise many to learn that Paul and the other writers of the New Testament identify *only two* activities that are prescribed for the church on Sunday. These two activities are only mentioned in two passages of Scripture. That tells us (1) there are no other activities that are required, and that (2) these activities are essential. The first is the passage quoted above (1 Cor. 16:2), and it relates to a regular procedure for grace giving. The second passage is Acts 20:7a, which states, "On the first day of the week, when we were gathered together to break bread." This verse describes the regular Sunday meeting of the members of the body of Christ for worship, fellowship and teaching.

In order to put this in perspective and relate it to our grace giving, we need to recall that the importance of the "first day of the week" (properly identified by many as "the Lord's Day") is derived from the fact that it was on that day Christ's resurrection took place (Lk. 24:1–9). We know that Christ's resurrection confirmed all that the love and grace of God the Father and God the Son had promised, and provided the basis for the beginning of the newly created body of Christ at Pentecost. Therefore, on the Lord's Day (1) we come collectively as members of the body of Christ to glorify Him and His grace through worship and fellowship, and (2) we come individually as new creations in Christ to glorify Him and His grace through our expression of generous grace giving. God has designed this gracious plan wherein we are able to be regularly blessed and strengthened by our worship and fellowship with our brothers and sisters in Christ while being individually fulfilled by the benefits and delights of grace giving.

This establishes the principle: *Our giving should be a personal matter for everyone that is both a privilege and a responsibility (1 Cor. 16:1–2).* It is not optional, and remember how God purposely extended the privilege of grace giving to the poverty-stricken Macedonians. Giving is a personal matter by which every believer is enabled to tangibly express their love for God. No one else needs to know how much we give because grace giving takes place in the presence of our omniscient and omnipresent Heavenly Father who knows the intents of our hearts and our giving is for His glory.

With the words "as he may prosper" (16:2), Paul points to the important principle that *giving is to be proportionate to what we receive.* This principle leads to a follow-up principle— *proportionate giving requires a weekly, personal, Spirit-directed evaluation and assessment of how much we have received in order to determine how much we should "put aside and save" to have available to disburse (1 Cor. 16:2).* This assessment is a personal matter and will undoubtedly differ in amount, percentage, or total for every individual. One fact we must recognize is that no New Testament precepts or principles of giving include any rules specifying amounts or percentages for giving.

Significant confusion exists in this regard since various concepts of tithing are practiced by the majority of Bible-believing churches and organizations identifying specific amounts or percentages for giving. This results when Old Testament tithing, designed by God in the Mosaic Law for the nation of Israel, has been improperly applied to the New Testament church and becomes a confusing substitute for Spirit-directed grace giving. Perhaps our awareness of the seriousness of this error, and the extent of its negative impact on congregational and personal stewardship, can be more clearly understood by reflecting on the following comments on this subject:

> Curiously, Paul, the New Testament writer who spoke most frequently on the topic of giving, never mentioned tithing. He had plenty of opportunities to explain this custom, because many of his readers were Gentiles who were unfamiliar with Jewish traditions. But since neither he nor any other New Testament writer commanded believers to give 10 percent of their earnings, we can conclude that we aren't obligated to tithe. Instead, we have the opportunity to give as the Lord lays it on our hearts. Grace giving, not tithing, is the task God has given us.[39]

Another author comments on the significance of this fact when he says, "Paul never used the word 'tithe' when he discussed giving, even though he gave more attention to giving than any other New Testament writer."[40]

In all probability most of us have never been inclined to question the issue of tithing before now. That's certainly understandable since various forms of tithing are so widely taught and practiced as the proper method of giving a Christian should follow today. In fact, it has been done so convincingly that even unbelievers often conclude that ten percent is what Christians are supposed to give to the church.

---

[39] Lawrence O. Richards, as cited by Charles Swindoll, *Calm Answers for a Confused Church* (Fullerton, CA: Insight for Living, 1988), 76.

[40] David K. Lowery, "2 Corinthians," in *The Bible Knowledge Commentary*, ed. John F. Walvoord and Roy B. Zuck (Wheaton, IL: Victor Books, 1983), 546.

However, according to one recent survey, the median annual giving for an American Christian is actually $200.00, just over half a percent of after-tax income.[41] According to another study, the mean aggregate donation over the course of a year given by those who regularly attend church is $1,548.00.[42] When you consider that the median household income in the United States during the period of the survey was $51,939.00,[43] the average level of giving was three percent of their income per household. So it appears that the method taught by many churches may not really be consistently practiced, especially since most, if not all Christians in our affluent culture easily spend much more than ten percent each year on vacations, cruises, recreational trips, sporting events, the latest gadgets and conveniences, not to mention things like newer or more cars than are needed or larger or more homes than are needed and the list could go on. The reality is that most of us could divest ourselves of a significant amount of nonessential things, including maintenance, planning, etc. without being inconvenienced or significantly deprived. In the end we could easily find much more discretionary wealth, time and freedom for giving and serving our gracious giving God.

Listen to someone who has extensively addressed this subject:

> Every believer owes 100 percent of what he is and what he has to God. The question, then, is not only

[41] Rob Moll, "Scrooge Lives!" *Christianity Today* (December 5, 2008), 24. Cited in Aubrey Malphurs, *The Nuts and Bolts of Church Planting* (Grand Rapids, MI: Baker Books, 2011), 261.

[42] George Barna and David Kinnaman, *Churchless* (Tyndale, 2014), 135.

[43] Accessed on July 6, 2015 at https://www.census.gov/content/dam/ Census/ library/ publications /2014/demo /p60-249.pdf, p. 5.

how much I give, but also how much I spend on myself. *Proportionate giving alone can furnish the right answer to this matter and for every stage of life.* We give because He gave, not because He commanded; we give because we want to, not because we have to; we give because we love Him, and we show that love most concretely in this way. If in turn God blesses us materially, we praise Him; if not, we still praise Him. This is grace giving, and this is the proof of our love for God.[44]

In addition, the following observations further support the fact that tithing is not designed by God as the methodology for grace giving in His church.

As we think about this issue in regard to the biblical record, it is significant that Paul and the New Testament writers never mentioned tithing as a principle, precept or Spirit-directed command related to grace giving. During that same time however, they did find it repeatedly necessary to correct attempts by some churches and converted Jewish Christians to bring in such things as dietary restrictions and circumcision from the Mosaic Law and impose them particularly on Gentile believer's and churches. In fact, these issues became so problematic, that the apostles and prophets (foundational leaders, Eph. 2:20–22) of the churches met in the Jerusalem Counsel, agreed to the correction of these errors and send a letter to all of the churches with directions

---

[44] Those are the words of Dr. Charles Ryrie in *Balancing the Christian Life* (Chicago, IL: Moody Press, 1969), 89. No one has dealt with the confusing issue of tithing more completely, correctly, clearly, and concisely than he has. His extended explanation is contained in Appendix A of this book. We encourage everyone to study his material.

to cease such practices (Acts. 15:1–35). It is both helpful to our consideration, and somewhat ironic that as Moses gave the Nation of Israel his final review of the Law, and defined both (1) the dietary laws and (2) tithing laws in one chapter (Deut. 14). The Jerusalem Counsel corrected the dietary issues, but made no mention of any need to correct incidents of tithing being inappropriately applied to grace giving by any of the early congregations. Nor was such an imposition of tithing even made a part of proportionate giving all through the Spirit's instructions for grace giving.

Then consider the fact that according to the Mosaic Law tithing was not giving, but paying. In fact, there were actually three tithes with prescribed percentage rates, which would have resulted in an Israelite family giving nineteen percent of their annual income to the Lord. Furthermore, payment was required, and there were judgmental consequences for failing to pay. This was a compulsory tax-and-pay system that God appropriately designed for the nation of Israel as a theocracy, and it clearly does not coincide with His amazing design of Spirit directed grace giving for the New Testament Spirit-indwelt body of Christ.

Finally, it is obvious that giving in the New Testament is different than in the Old Testament because the ultimate expression of giving was personified by God Himself when the Father gave His Son, who then gave His life for our redemption. When His Son rose from the dead and ascended, He gave the Holy Spirit to indwell us. Considering all that God owns and has entrusted to us, whether it be material resources, talents and abilities, or time, Jesus said, "Freely you received, freely give" (Matt. 10:8) and James tells us "Every good thing given and every perfect gift is from above, coming down from the

Father of lights, with whom there is no variation or shifting shadow" (Jam. 1:17). In the passage we've been examining (1 Cor. 16:1–2), Paul reminds us that God has provided grace giving as an instrument whereby we can show our gratitude to Him. In principle: *Our grace giving accurately measures our gratitude to God.*

> Christian giving is a grace, the outflow of the grace of God in our lives and not the result of promotion or pressure. An open heart cannot maintain a closed hand. If we appreciate the grace of God extended to us, we will want to express that grace by sharing it with others.[45]

Another author writes concerning this passage:

> "Let each one"—that's us. "Just as he has purposed"— or planned. The Greek term for *purposed* means "to choose beforehand, to decide ahead of time." This planning should originate not from external pressures but from within, "in his heart." Gracious giving is the result of heartfelt resolve. If it isn't from the heart, it is given "grudgingly or under compulsion." But when giving is from the heart full of cheer, it evokes not only the attention of God but also His love.[46]

Now In order to complement his instructions in 1 Corinthians 16:2, let's return to 2 Corinthians 9:7, where

---

[45] Warren Wiersbe, *Be Wise* (Wheaton, IL: Victor Books, 1983), 163.
[46] Charles Swindoll, *A Minister Everyone Would Respect* (Fullerton, CA: Insight for Living, 1989), 27.

Paul is urging the Corinthians to complete their offering for the Jerusalem saints, just as they had responded to the Spirit's direction at the beginning, by saying, "Each one must do just as he has purposed in his heart, not grudgingly or under compulsion, for God loves a cheerful giver." Paul knew that they had readiness, zeal, enthusiasm and were contagiously cheerful at the beginning (9:2), but he also knew that the complications of their delay could negatively impact their attitude as they endeavored to complete the project. What he wanted them to understand was that since their giving began with a Spirit-directed heart, it should not be finished grudgingly or under compulsion. *God's design for grace giving includes cheerfulness and God's love for the giver (2 Cor. 9:7).*

To convince the Corinthians how the completion of their "previously promised bountiful gift" (9:5) without further hindrance or delay could indeed come to pass, Paul encourages them to apply the biblical principle of sowing and reaping as he quotes "he who sows sparingly will also reap sparingly, and he who sows bountifully will also reap bountifully" (9:6). Then by adding in principle the truth that *material seed may reap a spiritual harvest (9:9)*, plus God's promise "Now He who supplies seed to the sower and bread for food will supply and multiply your seed for sowing and increase the harvest of your righteousness" (9:10), Paul confirms that gracious principle that *the more we generously give to others the more God enriches us (2 Cor. 9:10).* In other words, just as the Macedonians were enriched, so we and the Corinthians will be enriched with every generous grace giving experience. Paul assures us of this fact with these words:

you will be enriched in everything for all liberality, which through us is producing thanksgiving to God. For the ministry of this service is not only fully supplying the needs of the saints, but is also overflowing through many thanksgivings to God. Because of the proof given by this ministry, they will greatly glorify God for your obedience to your confession of the gospel of Christ and for the liberality of your contribution to them and to all, while they also by prayer on your behalf, yearn for you because of the surpassing grace of God in you. (9:11–14)

Paul is describing the principle that *our pure, Spirit-directed grace giving must come from a genuine attitude of selflessness that can only be the result of the surpassing grace of God in us (2 Cor. 9:14).* This character quality was beautifully displayed by the Macedonians (8:1–4), as it had been epitomized in the life and death of our Lord Jesus Christ (8:9). Paul is telling the Corinthians that by generously completing their promised giving they would be displaying that same character quality because of the surpassing grace of God in them. We can experience the same as we engage in generous grace giving.

What a magnificent picture of God's surpassing grace the body of Christ displays when (1) saints minister to and care for one another through grace giving, (2) offer praise and thanksgiving to God for His gracious provision of material and spiritual blessings, and (3) intercede for one another, (4) all for the glory of God (9:14). For here we see the principle that *God is glorified when we graciously give, because it's done without seeking credit for ourselves. God is also glorified when we receive gracious gifts and realize how unworthy and undeserving we are (2 Cor. 9:14).*

This key passage (2 Cor. 8:1—9:14) began with grace (8:1) and concludes with grace (9:15, the Greek word for "grace" is translated "thanks" in this context and means "to bestow favor"). As incredible as it may seem to think that we could bestow favor on God, and the only reason we can love as God loves is because He first loved us. Then with that same love we can love Him and one another (1John 4:7–21). In like manner we are able to bestow favor on God because of the countless favors He has bestowed on us. We can do that by bestowing the favor of glory, adoration, worship, submission, and endless praise for the greatest favor He bestowed on us in the gift of His Son. We can also bestow on God the favor of submission to the Spirit's direction to bestow His favor of generous grace giving in meeting the needs of others. Indeed we are richly blessed by His eternal love and amazing grace.

We must add that the Corinthians did complete their generous gracious work. Paul informs us of that fact in Romans 15:25–27, when he said:

> but now I am going to Jerusalem serving the saints. For Macedonia and Achaia [that's Corinth] have been pleased to make a contribution for the poor among the saints in Jerusalem. Yes, they were pleased to do so and they are indebted to them. For if the Gentiles have shared in their spiritual things, they are indebted to minister to them also in material things.

It is encouraging and refreshing to learn that the Corinthians followed the Spirit's direction through to completion of their gracious work. But we must not overlook Paul's last sentence where he points out the important connection between spiritual things and material things. We have seen this from the very beginning of our study when we learned that a continuing pursuit of godly living with total dependence upon the Spirit's direction and enablement is essential for engaging in grace giving while storing up future eternal treasures.

This perspective has many ramifications, but as we conclude our presentation of individual and corporate stewardship of material resources within the body of Christ, two particular facts should help us grasp how the stewardship of talents and abilities, or time relate. First, our exercise of Spirit-directed grace giving is ministry or service that is equally as important as another person's exercise of Spirit-directed teaching or pastoring, because both actions accomplish the will of God in keeping with each individual's giftedness and obedience. Second, in most of our Spirit-directed ministry or service, our stewardship responsibilities overlap or are intertwined. This is due to the reality that most precepts, principles, and guidelines are identical or similar for all three areas of stewardship, i.e. our foundational principles. Again, the key is diligence in our pursuit of godly living with contentment so that our trustworthy stewardship in all areas becomes a growing and fulfilling life-style, as we are continually becoming what God wants us to become. These distinct aspects will become increasingly evident as we expand our presentation of God-given opportunities to include the stewardship of talents and abilities, and time.

Summary Principles from 2 Corinthians 8:1—9:15

If we are going to know and do the will of God we must *first* give ourselves to God. The Spirit's control enables us to resist the influence of the world, the flesh and Satan in the decision making process and the Spirit's power enables godly behavior beyond our natural ability (8:2–5, p. 91).

God has granted the regular privilege and responsibility of giving to every believer whether wealthy or poor (2 Cor. 8:2–5; 1 Cor. 16:1–2, p. 92).

The assurance of God's promised supply instills total confidence for Spirit-directed giving since we know that God will meet every material need we have regardless of any circumstances created in obeying His will (2 Cor. 8:3, pp. 92-93).

It is our trust in God that enables us to give *when* the Spirit directs in keeping with *what* God has already provided (2 Cor. 8:10–12, p. 96).

Financial matters should be administered honestly, expediently, orderly and openly by people with spiritual maturity and tested ministry experience (2 Cor. 8:19–23, p. 99).

God provides all that is needed for the expedient beginning and completion of every Spirit directed task (2 Cor. 9:1–2, p. 100).

Proportionate giving requires a weekly, personal, Spirit-directed evaluation and assessment of how much we have received in order to determine how much we should put aside and save to have available to disburse (1 Cor. 16:2, p. 103).

Our grace giving accurately measures our gratitude to God (1 Cor. 16:1-2, p. 108).

God's design for grace giving includes cheerfulness and God's love for the giver (2 Cor. 9:7, p. 109).

The sowing of material seed reaps a spiritual harvest (2 Cor. 9:9, p. 109).

The more we generously give to others the more God enriches us (2 Cor. 9:10, p. 109).

Our pure Spirit-led grace giving must come from a genuine heart attitude of selflessness that can only be the result of the surpassing grace of God in us (2 Cor. 9:14, p. 110).

God is glorified when we graciously give, because it's done without seeking credit for ourselves and God is glorified when we receive gracious gifts and realize how unworthy and undeserving we are (2 Cor. 9:14, pp. 110-11).

CHAPTER 7

Stewardship of Talents and Abilities: How to live as those who belong to God (Part 1: Aquila and Priscilla)

Our objective in this section is to identify the biblical concept of *stewardship of talents and abilities* and explain the related biblical precepts, principles, and guidelines in a way that every Christian engaged in the pursuit of godly living can grasp and effectively apply them as the Spirit directs and enables. Though we presented the stewardship of material resources first, we will now show how the stewardship of talents and abilities represents the umbrella stewardship that touches virtually every area of our total life experience. In fact, as we observe the interaction of all three areas of stewardship, and recognize how the Holy Spirit uses them in tandem in us as individuals and among the members of the body of Christ, the love and grace of our sovereign heavenly Father are amazingly displayed. The example of two of Paul's close friends and coworkers—Aquila and Priscilla— warrants our attention at this point because it can provide fresh inspiration and insight for developing our trustworthy stewardship.

The record of Aquila and Priscilla opens with Luke's description of Paul's arrival in Corinth in Acts 18:1–3.

> After these things he [Paul] left Athens and went to Corinth. And there he found a Jew named Aquila, a native of Pontus, having recently come from Italy with his wife Priscilla, because Claudius had commanded all Jews to leave Rome. He came to them, and because he was of the same trade, he stayed with them and they were working, for by trade they were tent-makers.

From this brief description we learn that Aquila and Priscilla were Jewish tent-makers who had moved to Corinth because the Roman Emperor Claudius had commanded all Jews to leave Rome. When Paul met them, they had been in Corinth long enough to secure a home and set up their business. They had probably heard about Jesus during their time in Rome, but Luke does not mention their conversion before coming to Corinth. We can only assume that Paul would naturally explore options for living quarters with Jews since it was his practice to begin his ministry in the synagogue every Sabbath upon arrival in a city.

What we do learn for certain is that their common vocation of tent-making initiated the business and housing relationship that continued for over eighteen months, during the time Paul established the Corinthian congregation with Aquila and Priscilla becoming prominent members. One commentator aptly describes it this way, "Although they at first associated with one another for business reasons, Paul's employers soon became the most devoted Christians and the closest friends of the apostle."[47] In fact, so confirmed was their conversion security, so effectively did they grow spiritually through Paul's teaching (including everything he covered in his first letter to the Corinthians) and discipling that when Paul moved on to Ephesus, they were led by the Spirit to go with him, business and all, to assist in the planting of a church in Ephesus (Acts 18:18–21).

Though there is more to the story, we need to pause here and notice how Paul handled the stewardship of his vocation in meeting and establishing a relationship with Aquila and Priscilla. The biblically designed purpose for the Christian's vocation is directed toward three objectives in our ministry of stewardship. *First* of all, our vocation, like every other area of our life, is a platform for God and others to observe. *Second*, God uses it to provide our essential material needs. *Third*, God provides the amount of discretionary wealth He chooses to entrust to us with as trustworthy stewards in keeping with the foundational principle of distribution. In other words, the manner in which we fulfill our vocational responsibilities should reflect the character of Christ and display the fruit of the Spirit in every dimension of our activity and attitude—including our learning to be content and our willingness to genuinely distinguish between needs and wants in ministering to others.

With the successful founding of the Corinthian church, plus Paul's incredible impact in the lives of Aquila and Priscilla, it is clear that he excelled in fulfilling all of these objectives. In fact, by supporting himself with his own discretionary wealth earned through his vocation, he went beyond expectations

---

[47] R. C. H. Lenski, *The Interpretation of The Acts of the Apostles* (Minneapolis, MN: Augsburg Publishing House, 1961), 746.

with regard to the remuneration he could have claimed from the Corinthian congregation, but graciously refused, so as not to appear to take advantage of privileges that were rightly his (1 Cor. 9:1–14; 1Tim. 5:17–18).

To continue our account of the spiritual growth of Aquila and Priscilla as recorded in Acts 18:19–22 we learn that when they arrived in Ephesus, Paul in his usual fashion entered the synagogue and reasoned with the Jews (18:19b). When they asked him to stay for a longer time, he declined but assured them that he intended to return. He did however, leave Aquila and Priscilla in Ephesus to minister while he left on an extended journey to the churches in Jerusalem and Antioch (18:20–22).

Luke says that during Paul's lengthy absence,

> a Jew named Apollos, an Alexandrian by birth, an eloquent man, came to Ephesus, and he was mighty in the Scriptures. This man had been instructed in the way of the Lord, and being fervent in spirit, he was speaking and teaching accurately the things concerning Jesus, being acquainted only with the baptism of John [the Baptist]. (18:24–25)

It is important to note the outstanding credentials Luke ascribes to Apollos. For example, he had been born and highly educated in Alexandria, Egypt. That city had a large Jewish population, many of whom had responded to the ministry of the disciples of John the Baptist by receiving the baptism of repentance and accepting Jesus as the crucified and risen Savior and Messiah. Most importantly, Luke says that "he was mighty in the Scriptures" (18:24b), which meant that he spoke and taught the Old Testament prophetic truths about Christ accurately and was fervent in declaring this message to his fellow Jews. Apollos had evidently heard some of the facts of the ministry of Christ, but had not learned the whole story, perhaps the ascension, but particularly the coming of the Holy Spirit at Pentecost, the beginning of the church, and believers' baptism by the Spirit into the body of Christ.

As Luke continues he describes the spiritual maturity of Priscilla and Aquila when he writes, "...and he [Apollos] began to speak out boldly in the synagogue. But when Priscilla and Aquila heard him, they took him aside and explained to him the way of God more accurately" (18:26). Now don't miss the dynamic that happened when two business people, converted, thoroughly taught and personally discipled under Paul's ministry in Corinth, took Apollos aside one day and expounded the Christian message to him more thoroughly.

> It was highly providential that this valuable man came to Ephesus just at this time. The teachers he needed to complete his education had also been providentially brought to Ephesus just at this time. Paul was not there and would not get there for some time. Not even a congregation was found there. Only a humble tent-maker and his equally unpretentious wife were there to take Apollos in hand. But would this eloquent, able university graduate condescend to go to school to a common artisan, and to his wife who had never attended a university? We shall see. The best university training Apollos ever received was given him in this tent-maker's shop.... And among the greatest services these two ever rendered for the Lord

was what they did for Apollos. In the whole story of Acts there is no picture that is more ideal than this of Apollos and Aquila and his wife. [48]

Hence, as good stewards of their time, Priscilla and Aquila took the necessary time both to listen to Apollos speak and to meet with him privately (18:26). As good stewards of their knowledge of Scripture, as well as the ability to clearly explain biblical truth, they were able to correct Apollos' incomplete understanding of Christian baptism (18:26). As yielded to the indwelling Holy Spirit, their words were kind and persuasive, and able to direct Apollos without crushing his spirit or alienating a brother in Christ. In fact, the Spirit used Priscilla and Aquila as His instruments to make Apollos even more effective in the cause of Christ—in that "he greatly helped those who had believed" and "powerfully refuted the Jews in public, demonstrating by the Scriptures that Jesus was the Christ" (18:28).

This is the ideal display of God's grace at work in Christians pursuing godly living with contentment as trustworthy stewards of material resources, talents and abilities, or time for the glory of God, who were continually engaged in the process of becoming what God wanted them to be. Paul modeled it, Aquila and Priscilla caught it and began to model it for others—just as Paul had written when he said, "The things you have learned and received and heard and seen in me, practice these things, and the God of peace will be with you" (Phil. 4:9). And we should respond in the same way as we have opportunity.

---

[48] R. C. H. Lenski, *The Interpretation of The Acts of the Apostles* (Minneapolis, MN: Augsburg Publishing House, 1961), 770.

The final postscript written by Paul three to four years later in his letter to the Christians in Rome reads, "Greet Prisca and Aquila, my fellow workers in Christ Jesus, who for my own life risked their own necks, to whom not only do I give thanks, but also all the churches of the Gentiles; also greet the church that is in their house" (Rom. 16:3–5a). This shows that they didn't stop pursuing godly living with contentment for the glory of God—but continued to minister and be models to their brothers and sisters in the body of Christ.

Summary Principles from the Lives of Aquila and Priscilla

Our vocation, like every other area of our life, is a platform for God and others to observe (Acts 18:1–4, p. 117).

God uses our vocation to provide our essential material needs as well as to provide discretionary wealth (Acts 18:1–3, p. 117).

The manner in which we fulfill our vocational responsibilities should reflect the character of Christ and display the fruit of the Spirit in every dimension of our activity and attitude—including our learning to be content and our willingness to genuinely distinguish between needs and wants in order to minister to others (Acts 18:18–21, p. 117).

CHAPTER 8

Stewardship of Talents and Abilities: How to live as those who belong to God (Part 2: The Christian's Relationship to the Holy Spirit)

We now turn our attention to the precepts, principles and guidelines that directly relate to the stewardship of talents and abilities. The very things that Aquila and Priscilla introduced to Apollos about the Holy Spirit's prominent role in the Church is precisely the body of truth we need to explore and assimilate in order to understand and properly respond to this stewardship. You may remember that this relates directly to our *foundational principle of enablement:* "The Holy Spirit's permanent indwelling of every Christian, that began on the day of Pentecost, is the major distinctive of the church that set the body of Christ apart from any other body of believers in the past" (p. 43). When we add this additional sentence: "Anything done apart from depending upon the Holy Spirit is the work of the flesh and cannot glorify God," it seems only logical and necessary that our discussion of the stewardship of talents and abilities should center around our relationship with, our submission to, and our worship of

God the Holy Spirit who has taken up residence within us for the purpose of accomplishing the will of God in us, to us, and through us for His glory.

The Holy Spirit's Work in Salvation

A large portion of the Holy Spirit's ministry today relates to our salvation and results in unique benefits and privileges for every believer. But before we dig into those specifics, we need to observe a brief sketch of related events that help us understand and appreciate all that God has undertaken in establishing the completely new entity we know as the church of Jesus Christ or the body of Christ in which the Holy Spirit plays the key role. This all really began to unfold when Christ met with His disciples in the Upper Room the night before He was crucified (John 13:1—17:26). He told them many things about His departure and the coming of the Holy Spirit that they did not understand at the time, though He promised them, "These things I have spoken to you while I am with you, but the Helper, the Holy Spirit, whom the Father will send in My name, He will teach you all things, and bring to your remembrance all that I said to you" (14:25–26). In other words, all that He taught them about the Holy Spirit's future ministry would be true not only for the disciples, but for every member of the body of Christ in whom the Spirit permanently indwells individually and corporately. In fact, just a short time later He said "But I tell you the truth, it is to your advantage that I go away, for if I do not go away, the Helper will not come to you, but if I go, I will send Him to you" (16:7).

It is vitally important to connect these words with the command that the resurrected Christ gave His followers on the day of His ascension.

> Gathering them together, He commanded them not to leave Jerusalem, but to wait for what the Father had promised, "Which," He said, "you have heard from Me; for John baptized with water, but you will be baptized with the Holy Spirit not many days from now." (Acts 1:4–5)

This is the same promise He had mentioned in the Upper Room. If you've never read John 13:1—17:26 in conjunction with Acts 1:1—2:47 from this perspective, we would strongly encourage that you take the time to do so. It not only explains the dramatic change experienced by Peter, the other apostles, and all of the believers, but encourages us to pursue all that the indwelling Holy Spirit desires to accomplish through our submission to Him and the will of God, particularly as we pursue our trustworthy stewardship of life.

It was ten days later, on the day of Pentecost, when all the believers were gathered together, that the same promise was fulfilled and God the Holy Spirit, at that very moment began His ministry in, to, and through every believer. That incident marked the beginning of a new and unique relationship between God and all believers at the moment of our spiritual birth. This fact provides the basis for the challenging principle: *To make certain we fully discover and exercise all of the incredible benefits and privileged responsibilities God has entrusted to us for our trustworthy stewardship of talents and abilities as members of the body of Christ.*

The Convicting Work of the Holy Spirit

God extended His marvelous grace through the Spirit even before we were saved. In fact, it touched us when we were lost in sin, totally lacking in righteousness, and facing eternal judgment. The convicting work of the Spirit was taught by Jesus in His Upper Room when He said, "He, when He comes will convict the world concerning sin and righteousness and judgment" (John 16:8). A more complete, yet adequately concise explanation can usually be found in a good study Bible. One such definition is

> To convict means to set forth the truth of the gospel in such a clear light that men are able to accept it or reject it intelligently; i.e. to convince men of the truthfulness of the gospel. The Spirit will help break down the indifference of the typical pagan who has no conviction of sin, who holds a low regard for righteousness, and who pays no heed to warnings of the coming judgment.[49]

In addition to loving us enough to give His only Son to provide our salvation (John 3:16), God extended His grace by giving His Holy Spirit to make it possible for us to accept that gift together with the eternal life it provided.

In so doing the Spirit accomplished two things. First, He clearly affirmed that our salvation is all the work of God. In fact we learned that we were not seeking God, but His Spirit sought us and found us, verifying the Scriptures when they

---

[49] Charles C. Ryrie, *The Ryrie Study Bible* (Chicago, IL: Moody Press, 1978), note on John 16:8.

declare, "There is none righteous, not even one; there is none who understands, there is none who seek for God" (Rom. 3:10–11) and "You did not choose Me but I chose you, and appointed you, that you should go and bear fruit, and that your fruit would remain" (John 15:16). Second, He appointed us to join Him as messengers in the great work of evangelism. Consequently, when we combine our assignment to use our talents and abilities as messengers and the truth that only the Holy Spirit can convict and convince the unsaved to accept Christ we formulate our privileged stewardship principle: *That with every bit of talent, ability, and enablement the Spirit provides, we must zealously engage in our sole responsibility to (1) clearly and accurately communicate the gospel with our lips, (2) consistently display its presence in our daily activities, and (3) continually pray that the Holy Spirit will be pleased to use it to convict and convince the unsaved to accept Christ.*

The Regenerating Work of the Holy Spirit

When we come into the world we are physically alive, but because we are sinful from the moment of conception (Ps. 51:5), we are spiritually dead and estranged from God "for the wages of sin is death" (Rom. 6:23a). Therefore we need to be regenerated, or spiritually born, again as Jesus explained to Nicodemus, "That which is born of the flesh is flesh, and that which is born of the Spirit is spirit. Do not be amazed that I said to you, 'You must be born again'" (John 3:6–7). The moment we placed our faith in Christ for salvation, regeneration occurred, which means that we were immediately born again of the Spirit. We received eternal life (John 3:16) and became a child of God (John 1:12). Though faith and regeneration are closely related and take place at the same time, they are two distinct concepts. While faith is the human response to conviction and is the channel through which God's grace is received, regeneration is the supernatural work of God the Holy Spirit that imparts eternal life in us. Since *eternal* life began the moment we were born again, we are eternally secure.

We need to explore the depths of this quickening work of the Spirit in our effort to grasp all God has endowed us with by this magnificent transaction that Paul so vividly spells out in Ephesians 2:4–7, when he says:

> But God, being rich in mercy, because of His great love with which He loved us, even when we were dead in our transgressions, *made us alive* together with Christ (by grace you have been saved), and *raised us up with Him, and seated us with Him* in heavenly places in Christ Jesus, so that in the ages to come He might show the surpassing riches of His grace in kindness toward us in Christ Jesus.

God's instantaneous, supernatural, and creative work of regeneration is the foundation for all the Christian's experience and is utterly foreign to the natural man. But since our old nature with its raging capacity to serve self is not eradicated at conversion, it is important to know that regeneration imparts the new nature Paul describes as "a new creation" (2 Cor. 5:17) that actually brings a new capacity whereby we can overcome the old nature and serve righteousness. Perhaps we should conclude our brief discussion of regeneration by adapting Paul's conclusion as He expresses God's purpose for it and identifies our stewardship of talents and abilities principle: "For we are His workmanship, created in Christ Jesus for good works, which God prepared beforehand so that we would walk in them" (Eph. 2:10). The application of this principle takes on even deeper meaning and significance with this explanation:

> This verse beginning with *For* tells why this salvation is not from man or by his works. The reason is that salvation is *God's workmanship.* The word *"workmanship,"* ...denotes *a work of art or a masterpiece.* It differs from human "works" in Eph. 2:9. *Believers are God's workmanship* because they have been created (a work only God can do) in Christ Jesus. The purpose of this creation is that believers will do good works. *God's workmanship* is not achieved by good works, but it is to result in good works.[50]

The Indwelling Work of the Holy Spirit

In His Upper Room teaching session with the disciples, Jesus predicted:

> He [the Father] will give you another Helper that He may be with you forever; that is the Spirit of truth, whom the world cannot receive, because it does not see Him or know Him, but you know Him because He abides with you and will be in you. (John 14:16–17)

---

[50] Harold Hoehner, "Ephesians," in *The Bible Knowledge Commentary*, ed. John F. Walvoord and Roy B. Zuck (Wheaton, IL: Victor Books, 1983), 624.

When that was fulfilled on the day of Pentecost, the Holy Spirit initiated the new and distinctive feature of His ministry, setting every believer today apart from believers of all previous ages. This indwelling is permanent. The obvious implication is that God's actual presence within us is a solemn motivation for moral and spiritual purity in every area of our lives.

This truth both establishes and confirms principles for application in our trustworthy stewardship of talents and abilities. For example, in dealing with immorality by Corinthian believers (1 Cor. 6:19–20), Paul identifies the principle: *Since our bodies are the temple of the Holy Spirit, it should motivate us to glorify God with our body through moral purity (1 Cor. 6:19–20).* And Jesus' promise that the Spirit will teach by guiding us into all the truth and disclosing to us what is to come (John 16:13) is a call to diligently apply and pursue all that is available through the *Foundational Principle of Spiritual Growth.* Finally, as we face on one hand the continual opposition of the world, the flesh, and Satan, and on the other hand the universal indwelling of every member of the body of Christ, *the Foundational Principle of Spiritual Enablement* zealously applied provides the potential for victory over the enemy as well as (1) good works for the glory of God, (2) the benefit of our brothers and sisters in Christ, and (3) communicating the gospel to the unsaved.

The Baptizing Work of the Holy Spirit

When Paul wrote to the Corinthian believers to address many questions, improper behaviors, and serious spiritual issues, he communicated an amazing fact about every believer from the day of Pentecost until the completion of the body of Christ at the Rapture (1 Thess. 4:13–17) by declaring "For by one Spirit, we were all baptized into one body, whether Jews or Greeks, whether slaves or free, and we were all made to drink of one Spirit" (1 Cor. 12:13; cf. Acts 1:5, 11:16). This is the supernatural work of the Holy Spirit whereby He places every believer, without exception, into one body, that is the body of Christ, the church universal. This is not to be confused with water baptism, but it is a spiritual supernatural transaction that places us in a stewardship position with countless opportunities to manage the talents and abilities God has entrusted to us for the common good of the body of Christ and the glory of God.

The New Testament epistles are replete with descriptions, instructions and explanations regarding how His Body of believers is to accomplish God's will and purpose through our unity, diversity and interdependence as members. The major Bible passages addressing the issue are Romans 12:1-13, 1 Corinthians 12:1—14:40, and Ephesians 4:1-16. In these passages Paul sets forth a list of precepts and principles that adequately reflect the spirit of *the Foundational Principles of Balance, Spiritual Enablement,* and *Contentment* with which we will conclude our discussion of the baptism of the Holy Spirit. Recognizing the headship of Christ and the direction of the Spirit, Paul challenges the members of the body with these words:

> So as those who have been chosen of God, holy and beloved, put on a heart of compassion, kindness, humility, gentleness and patience; bearing with one another, and forgiving each other, whoever has a

complaint against anyone, just as the Lord forgave you, so also should you. Beyond all these things put on love, which is the perfect bond of unity. Let the peace of Christ rule in your hearts, to which indeed you were called in one body; and be thankful. Let the word of Christ richly dwell within you, with all wisdom teaching and admonishing one another with psalms and hymns and spiritual songs, singing with thanksgiving in your hearts to God. Whatever you do in word or deed, do all in the name of the Lord Jesus, giving thanks through Him to God the Father. (Col. 3:12–17)

The love, grace, and tender mercy of God in the believer that is vividly described in Paul's exhortation enriches our stewardship of talents and abilities within the body of Christ by the refreshing principle: *The effective accomplishment of the will of God reflects even more glory to Him when we, as gifted, unified, diverse, and interdependent members of the Body of Christ harmoniously express our firm commitment to godly living with attitudes and behavior bathed in a heart of compassion, kindness, humility, gentleness and patience.*

The Sealing Work of the Holy Spirit

The Sealing of the Holy Spirit is inseparably related to the indwelling of the Spirit and our *Foundational Principle of Ownership* because the word seal refers to a legal stamp or sign of ownership. As a result, the Holy Spirit is the seal God uses to claim His ownership and assure our confidence in eternal security. Convicting, regenerating, indwelling, baptism, and sealing are totally the work of God orchestrated by Him to coincide with the Holy Spirit's entrance at the moment of our salvation. Before we were consciously aware of how God responded to our faith, all of these ministries simultaneously occurred to provide everything we will ever need to know and experience regarding the good, acceptable and perfect will of God.

Now let's examine and analyze Paul's detailed description in Ephesians 1:13–14. It states:

> In Him, [Christ] you also, [Gentiles] after listening to the message of truth, the gospel of your salvation- [that's convicting] having also believed, [that's our faith] you were sealed [that's possession and security] in Him [Christ] with the Holy Spirit [that's the sealing; we are sealed by His presence] of promise [that's the Upper Room promise to the disciples recorded in Luke 24:49; John 14:16; 15:26; 16:13; Acts 1:5] who is given as a pledge [that's a deposit or down payment that guarantees full payment] of our inheritance [that's what Peter says is 'reserved for us in heaven' (1 Pet. 1:4)] with a view to the redemption [this Greek word for redemption used also in Eph. 4:30 refers to our ultimate release from the presence of sin which will take place at physical death or the Rapture] of God's own possession [we became God's own possession when we were released from the penalty of our sin by redemption, and that word is used in v. 7] to the praise of His glory [this needs to be repeated over and over as we experience the countless benefits of His great love, grace and mercy].

As we endeavor to take all of this in and try to imagine how we could ever conceive of an appropriate response, we would do well to consider the Person whose presence establishes God's secure ownership when Paul says "Do not grieve the Holy Spirit of God, by whom you were sealed for the day of redemption" (Eph. 4:30). The immediate context of the verses surrounding this admonition make it clear that our sins that grieve the Spirit begin with ungodly and insensitive thoughts and attitudes expressed first in speech and then in our behavior. Paul's exhortation has framed our principle: *Our sensitivity to the Person of the Holy Spirit, God's seal of ownership, should motivate us to employ every benefit He has provided, while completely depending upon His direction in order to keep from grieving Him by sinning (Eph. 4:30).*

The Holy Spirit's Work in the Christian's Daily Life

Our consideration of the work of the Holy Spirit in salvation explained what was primarily accomplished completely by God alone, beginning with conviction through to His setting in place the essential ingredients that guarantee our final arrival in heaven. Supernaturally it was all completed by Him the moment we placed our faith in Christ as our Savior and remains unchanged until our eternal life here on earth ends in death or the rapture. In fact, He was just completing what He had chosen to do before the foundation of the world (Eph. 1:1–14).

Notice how Dr. Dino Pedrone, internationally know Bible scholar, speaker, and currently president of Davis Bible

College, describes this in his recent book on Ephesians when he says:

> Look at verse 3, *"Blessed be the God and Father of our Lord Jesus Christ, who has blessed us with all spiritual blessings in heavenly places in Christ."* What you need, and what I need, we have in Christ.
>
> Don't ever pray, "God, give me more of Jesus." You received all there is when you got saved. Don't say "God, give me more of the Holy Spirit." You already have Him. We may need to submit to Him better and yield to Him better. But there is a great truth in this verse, that He has blessed us not with some spiritual blessings, but with all of them....
>
> Some people smile when they are going through hard times, and some people can't smile no matter what is going on.... God is saying, "Pull out that spiritual Social Security ID and see who you are in Christ." Let's see what the Father has done for us.
>
> Verse 4 says, *"Just as he chose us in him before the foundation of the world."* You ask, "Did God choose us?" Yes. If you want to know how He did it, let me give you a profound answer: I don't know. I used to think I knew, but I don't know how He does that.
>
> But I do know this. When He chose us, there was a reason. There was a purpose. Go back to verse 4. *"According as he hath chosen us in Him before the foundation of the world, that we should be holy and without blame before him in love."* Why did He choose us? He chose us to be holy and separated unto Him. We are to be blameless. So when God the Father looks at

you, and sees you in Christ, He sees you as if you had never committed a sin. He sees you as holy, without blame. Aren't you glad about that. We need to start trying to live that kind of life.[51]

An overview of the Spirit's accomplishments reveal that (1) we have eternal life, accompanied by all spiritual blessings; (2) the Holy Spirit lives within us forever; (3) we are permanent members of the church, the body of Christ that began on the day of Pentecost; (4) and the Holy Spirit who indwells us is God's stamp and seal of ownership, authority, and security so designed that no one but God could break the seal, and He has promised to keep us until our completed redemption delivers us from the presence of sin by Christ taking us to be with Him forever.

Our possession of this amazing, complete, and secure salvation qualifies us for entrance into heaven now, but our sovereign, loving, and gracious God, who always does what is right, has determined it best to leave us here in the world as His chosen servants and citizens of heaven, to accomplish His will and purpose through the Spirit's direction and enablement. The following examination of the Holy Spirit's work in our daily lives will focus primarily on our interaction with Him on the basis of His indwelling and our privileged function as members of the Body of Christ. Our objective is to identify, define, and explain any appropriate precepts and principles to which we should respond in the course pursuing godly living with contentment as trustworthy stewards.

---

[51] Dino Pedrone, *True ID: A Verse-by-Verse Study of Ephesians* (Xulon Press, 2008), 12-13.

The Holy Spirit Gives Spiritual Gifts

Except for one brief comment about spiritual gifts by Peter that we will touch on later, Paul is the primary New Testament writer who addresses this important subject, and he does so in great detail in three key passages—Romans 12:1-8; 1 Corinthians 12:1—14:39, and Ephesians 4:11-16. It is evident that Paul received from God a great deal of revelation about spiritual gifts and that he was zealous for every Christian to comprehend God's purpose for their implementation. In essence, Paul wants us to recognize that God endows every member of His church with these incredible tools for its effective functioning from founding to consummation.

To whet our appetites, you will recall that in 1 Corinthians 12:13, Paul says that every Christian has been placed into the body of Christ by the baptism of the Holy Spirit. But it is important to note that he also opens the same chapter with "Now concerning spiritual gifts, brethren, I do not want you to be unaware" (12:1), and then says "But to each one is given the manifestation [gift or gifts] of the Spirit for the common good" (12:7). With that in mind, consider also that in Romans 12:4-5 Paul says "we have many members in one body [that's unity] and all members do not have the same function [that's diversity], so we, who are many, are one body in Christ, and individually members one of another [that's interdependence]." To that Paul adds "Since we have gifts that differ according to the grace given to us, each of us is to exercise them accordingly" (12:6) as we minister to one another in the body of Christ.

Even though we have not yet defined spiritual gifts, let's first examine these two sets of verses in the context of the entire chapters where they appear, for as we do, we see that Paul has already taught us some things about spiritual gifts and identified principles that we need to apply. First, Paul wants us to recognize that spiritual giftedness is very important in regard to our effective functioning in the body of Christ. Thus we need to apply the principle: *We should learn all Paul has to teach us about spiritual gifts and their role in the body of Christ (1 Cor. 12:1, 13)*. Second, since we all have received spiritual gifts that are to be exercised in the body of Christ, we should apply the principle: *We need to learn how to discover, develop and exercise our spiritual gifts in the body of Christ as effectively as possible and fulfill our stewardship of abilities in a trustworthy manner (Rom. 12:6; 1 Cor. 12:7)*.

Since these principles can be applied immediately, let's begin by defining spiritual gifts. Much has been written about the subject of spiritual gifts with a variety of definitions, but in the final analysis this one is concise and conforms to sound biblical interpretation: *A spiritual gift is a God-given ability for service in the body of Christ.*[52] This definition accurately identifies the givers as Christ and the Holy Spirit, the meaning of gift as a divinely bestowed ability, and the purpose for the gifts as service in the body of Christ.

In our discussion, it will be helpful for us to keep in mind that we have (1) spiritual gifts which are essentially God-given abilities received at the time of conversion plus (2) God-given natural abilities received at physical birth, as well as (3) acquired abilities for which God's grace has provided related educational and vocational opportunities for development. Though the first is our primary focus, all three areas must

---

[52] Charles C. Ryrie, *Basic Theology* (Chicago, IL: Moody Press, 1999), 424.

be included in our total stewardship of abilities because all three can enrich the building up and edifying of the body of Christ when properly managed according to the Spirit's direction. To express this truth in principle: *God has endowed us with God-given spiritual abilities, God-given natural abilities, and God-given acquired abilities to be used for building up the body of Christ through the Spirit's directing and enabling our trustworthy stewardship of abilities.* We need to remember however, that spiritual gifts like evangelism or giving are essentially abilities that may employ natural or acquired abilities like singing or practicing medicine as vehicles or platforms, but they remain distinct from each other, because a spiritual gift is the ability itself, not the vehicle or platform. In like manner, the spiritual gift is an ability such as teaching, shepherding, faith, and showing mercy that are to be exercised in a local church—but can be used in multiple circumstances and conditions and should not to be defined by or limited to a location, an organizational position, or a certain age group.

Romans 12:6–8; 1 Corinthians 12:8–10, 28–30, and Ephesians 4:11 together provide us with what appears to be a complete list of spiritual gifts. The word "spiritual" is a derivative of the Greek word for grace and indicates that the gifts are another expression of the grace of God that "saved" us and "created us in Christ Jesus for good works" (Eph. 2:8–10). The gifts are called *spiritual* because they are distributed by the Holy Spirit, in conjunction with Christ, the ascended Head of the church, to each Christian sovereignly "as He wills" (1Cor. 12:11) in keeping with His choice of the particular gifts (12:8–10) and the needs of the body at any particular time or place. It is helpful to recognize the needs and timing aspects in the distribution of gifts, because it enables us to understand why some gifts that were exercised at one time or place in the Church are not exercised today. For example, the gift of apostleship and prophecy appear first in two lists (1 Cor. 12:37–38; Eph. 4:11) and the Scripture says that those gifts were given for laying the foundation of the church (Eph. 2:20). Ever since that work was completed, the Holy Spirit has continued to distribute gifts designed for the continual building up or edifying the church as Paul states "being built together into a dwelling of God in the Spirit" (Eph. 2:22). Notice also that the gifts of signs, wonders, and miracles were distributed by the Spirit and accompanied those who revealed and taught the foundational doctrines of the gospel and church. The gifts authenticated the messengers and the message for the first generation believers (Heb. 2:3–4).

One writer has explained these distribution adjustments this way,

> A gift given once is a gift given to the whole body of Christ...in the twentieth century we are still benefiting from and building on those foundational gifts. They were given in the first century to the whole body in all centuries. No generation has been slighted. The Spirit endows the church as He wills, and He knows exactly what each believer, each congregation, and each generation needs.[53]

---

[53] Charles C. Ryrie, *Basic Theology* (Chicago, IL: Moody Press, 1999), 369. For a thorough treatment of the distinction between temporary and permanent gifts, see Paul Enns, *The Moody Handbook of Theology*, Revised and Expanded Edition (Chicago, IL: Moody Press, 2008), 280-89, and Charles C. Ryrie, *The Holy Spirit*, Revised and Expanded (Chicago, IL: Moody Press, 1997), 129-54. For an excellent treatment of spiritual gifts

This gives an excellent insight as the basis for the principle: *As we positively respond to the Spirit's direction by taking every opportunity He provides to exercise the gifts He has given, we should do it zealously and with complete confidence that we are functioning as God's servants fulfilling God's purpose of building up the body of Christ in the right place at the right time.* This means the Holy Spirit places every member in the body of Christ according to His perfect plan and endows each of us with the perfect gift or gifts so that experiencing the good, pleasing, and perfect will of God is potentially available individually and corporately as we depend completely on His direction.

In all we have reviewed about spiritual gifts, it is clear that every member of the body of Christ has at least one gift, and perhaps more, but since we are to serve one another with our gifts it is improbable that anyone has all of the gifts. In his brief comments about spiritual gifts, Peter says,

> As each one has received a special gift, employ it in serving one another as good stewards of the manifold grace of God. Whoever speaks, is to do so as one who is speaking the utterances of God, whoever serves is to do so as one who is serving by the strength which God supplies, so that in all things God may be glorified through Jesus Christ, to whom belongs the glory and dominion forever and ever, Amen. (1 Pet. 4:10–11)

---

generally, see William McRae, *Dynamics of Spiritual Gifts* (Grand Rapids, MI: Zondervan Publishing House, 1976).

These words coincide with Paul's and are expressed in a passionate appeal. But the question still remains; how can we personally know which gifts are ours?

Since we know spiritual gifts have been given, and that we are expected to exercise them, and since there are no recorded verses or passages explaining how to discover ours, here are some suggestions. The first is to invest time and effort in *learning as much as we can from the Scriptures about spiritual gifts*. The disciplined study and application of biblical truth is one of the most important ingredients in the discovery process, as detailed in our *Foundational Principle of Spiritual Growth—but godly living with contentment can only be experienced as we continually engage in the pursuit of spiritual growth.*

Paul wrote that Christ "gave Himself for us to redeem us from every lawless deed, and to purify for Himself a people for His own possession, zealous for good deeds" (Titus 2:13). Based on this verse, the incredible cost Christ paid to make us His possession and committed servants during our remaining earthly life is clear. Such knowledge should instill a willingness to actively identify our spiritual gift and pursue any opportunity of service that could allow us to put it to effective use. Committed behavior resulting from such an attitude is the essence of our second suggestion. It is clear that Christ's example should remove any selfish consideration of the inconvenience, time, energy, risk, and even embarrassment involved in serving others. In addition, we know that it is much easier to direct a moving vehicle than a stationary one. In other words, the Spirit may be pleased to use our action to eliminate, redirect, or open an entirely new perspective regarding the discovery of our spiritual gift.

Responding to these suggestions reflects our genuine pursuit of godly living with contentment. It is reasonable to believe that in response to our pursuit to know God and do His will above all else, our final suggestion is that we trust the indwelling Holy Spirit who has given us gifts, to identify them for us, especially since He has given no specific steps in the Bible for discovery. Then, in concert with continually learning to be content, we must apply the principle: "Be anxious for nothing, but in everything by prayer and supplication with thanksgiving let your requests be made known to God. And the peace of God, which passes all comprehension, will guard your hearts and your minds in Christ Jesus" (Phil. 4:6-7) and trust Him to accomplish for us what we cannot accomplish for ourselves.

The Holy Spirit Fills

From the very moment the Church began and the Spirit commenced His permanent indwelling of believers, the history recorded in the book of Acts makes it clear that effective evangelism and building up the body of Christ is inseparably related to the filling of the Holy Spirit. This was confirmed at Pentecost (Acts 2) when Peter, who was Spirit-filled, or Spirit-controlled, stood up before the crowd of thousands and explained what God was doing. That sermon resulted in the conversion and baptism of about three thousand souls (2:41).

There is one other event that will give us a practical, everyday perspective on the filling of the Spirit. In Acts 6:1–7 a logistical problem had arisen that involved collecting and distributing supplies and funds for two sizable groups of newly saved widows and making sure neither group was being overlooked. In order to be certain this important ministry was properly handled, the apostles, in need of more time for prayer and ministering the Word, suggested that seven men with noble qualifications, including being filled with the Holy Spirit, be selected for this work (6:3–6). This was done with the approval of the entire congregation. Not only did this arrangement result in enhanced growth for the church (6:7), but the selection process tells us that the filling of the Holy Spirit (1) was clearly identifiable in the life of the filled believer, (2) was a common, ordinary characteristic for members of the early church, and (3) it was necessary in order to effectively exercise any one, or any combination of God-given spiritual, natural, and acquired abilities for service.

In discussing our pursuit of godly living with contentment, we have emphasized matters relating to filling such as submission to God and His will plus total dependence upon the Spirit in doing His will. In addition, the New Testament letters actually present the filling of the Holy Spirit as the necessary requirement for the Christian's daily spiritual growth and maturity. It is imperative therefore for us to turn our attention to this most important subject in order to correctly define and accurately understand what it is the Spirit wants to accomplish.

For our definition we must return to the passage where Paul tells us, "And do not get drunk with wine, for that is dissipation, but be filled with the Spirit" (Eph. 5:18). Notice first that Paul is addressing all of the believers of the Ephesian church with two specific commands, or precepts. God intends for all of us to obey these commands since they are not optional. And clearly, the comparison between drunkenness and the filling of the Spirit has to do with control. This means that the Spirit-filled life is a life no longer controlled by the flesh but by the Spirit.

Not only is the expression "be filled" a command, but the verb is in the present tense which requires continued or repeated action, and could well be translated "keep on being filled." Thus, unlike indwelling and baptism that are one-time, permanent acts, a Christian can be filled repeatedly. In fact, since the Spirit indwells us because He wants to fill us and we cannot fill ourselves, we could really use the translation "keep on letting the Spirit fill us." In other words, to be filled with the Spirit is to have the Spirit fulfilling all He came to do in the first place.

Since being filled by the Spirit is both an expected and obtainable requirement for the Christian life, what must we do in order to be filled? By failing to properly distinguish the baptism of the Spirit from the filling of the Spirit and the coming of the Spirit at Pentecost, many have determined that some form of waiting, tarrying, praying or pleading make up the proper prerequisites for the filling of the Spirit. The reality is however, that no directive or example of believers praying for the filling of the Spirit exists in the Scriptures. However, there are three conditions we must meet in order to be Spirit-filled that are identified by three specific commands—two negative and one positive.

"Quench not the Spirit"

The first command is expressed by Paul as he speaks to the young, model Thessalonian congregation. He had commended them for their strong desire to learn and do the will of God, and says "Do not quench the Spirit" (1 Thess.

5:19). By employing the analogy of fire, "quench" means to stifle or suppress the ministry of the Spirit in a believer or in a congregation. In this context "quench" relates to the believer's unwillingness to yield to the work of the indwelling Holy Spirit thereby resisting the will of God. When we do this we are being self-directed rather than Spirit-led. Therefore, the crucial word involved in obeying this command and meeting this condition is "yield," which requires total submission of self to God's will as a rule of life.

Yielding is commonly referred to as dedication. This is the desire of God expressed twice by Paul when he says, "Therefore I urge you, brethren, by the mercies of God, to present your bodies a living and holy sacrifice, acceptable to God, which is your spiritual service of worship" (Rom. 12:1), and "present yourselves to God as those alive from the dead, and your members as instruments of righteousness to God" (Rom. 6:13b). The passionate plea for dedication found in Romans 12:1 is based upon our belief that the overwhelming mercy, goodness, love, and grace of God so magnificently unfolded in Romans 1:1—11:36, and already received by us, is worthy of such a response. This is God's pattern as He richly blesses us in salvation by faith alone and then calls for obedience, commitment, and dedication. In fact, as ironic as it may seem, God never asks for a sacrifice without providing that sacrifice, which is precisely what this dedication is all about. In other words, on the basis of all that we are as new creatures in Christ, in addition to all that He has provided for this life and the life with Christ to come, God pleads with us to submit or dedicate ourselves to Jesus Christ and the indwelling Holy Spirit's control in order to effectively pursue the will of God as the rule of life.

The word translated "present" in both passages is in the Greek verbal form that should be translated, "present yourself or your bodies to God *once for all.*" Since we are to present (or yield) our "bodies a living and holy sacrifice," it follows that our dedication involves the remaining years of our life being set apart completely to Him and His will. Consequently, having already become Christians by receiving Christ as our Savior, all Christians pursuing godly living with contentment can avoid quenching the Spirit by dedication. This leads to the principle: *Following conversion, dedication is the most important decision we must make in order to answer the question of who's in charge or who will control the remainder of our earthly Christian life, and in so doing meet the prerequisite of once for all dedication as the initial condition for being filled with the Spirit (Rom. 12:1; 6:13).*

Needless to say, this is not an easy or hasty decision to make. It requires much in-depth consideration and assessment of all that is involved. The following words should provide greater insight.

> For who among man knows the thoughts of a man except the spirit of the man which is in him? Even so the thoughts of God no one knows except the Spirit of God. *Now we have received not the spirit of the world, but the Spirit who is from God, so that we may know the things freely given to us by God.* (1 Cor. 2:11–12, italics added)

Dr. Lewis S. Chafer writes:

> Nothing could be more misdirected than a self-directed life.... It is the divine plan that the element of

guidance shall be supplied in us by God Himself.... How much we feel we have gained when we can say, "Thy will, not mine be done!" It is because our daily life will be helpless and a failure apart from the leading of the Spirit, and because the Spirit has come to do this very work, that we cannot be rightly adjusted to Him, or be spiritual, until we are yielded to the mind and will of God.[54]

Later he adds:

Yielding to the will of God is not demonstrated by some particular issue; it is rather a matter of taking the will of God as the rule of one's life...without reference to any particular thing He may choose. It is electing His will to be final, even before we know what He may wish us to do.... it is a question of being willing to do anything.[55]

It certainly seems appropriate to adapt Dr. Chafer's words for expressing the principle: *Our yielding to the will of God is a matter of accepting it as the rule of life by electing it to be final even before we know what He may wish us to do, which means being willing to do anything.* Another writer adds:Yieldedness to the Spirit includes (1) submission to the plain teaching of the Word of God, (2) obedience to the guidance of the Spirit, and (3) acceptance in faith of the providential acts of God. All of these are a part of the moment-by-moment experience

---

[54] Lewis Sperry Chafer, *He That is Spiritual* (Grand Rapids, MI: Zondervan Publishing House, 1967), 87.
[55] *Ibid.*, 91.

of living in the will of God with an indwelling Spirit who is unquenched.[56]

"Grieve not the Spirit"

This second negative command is directed by Paul in his letter to one of the most mature, well taught congregations in the New Testament. It reads, "Do not grieve the Holy Spirit of God, by whom you were sealed for the day of redemption" (Eph. 4:30). At salvation, the permanent indwelling of the Spirit became our seal and stamp of God's ownership, establishing our bodies as the temple of God. This was described by Paul when he said, "Do you not know that you are a temple of God and that the Spirit of God dwells in you?... for the temple of God is holy and that is what you are" (1 Cor. 3:16, 17b). This means that we are new creatures in Christ, blessed to live every moment of our lives in vital union with the infinitely holy God who will never depart or withdraw because of our sin. As a result, He is understandably grieved when we sin, knowing that it will hinder and disrupt His effective work of enabling our continual pursuit of godly living with contentment and the trustworthy stewardship of our abilities and talents for His glory.

The need for this command is compounded by the reality that even when we have dealt with the sin of *quenching* the Spirit by dedication or determining once for all that God will, through the indwelling Holy Spirit's control, run our lives, our sin nature will not be removed until our earthly life ends and we are glorified. Our old nature constantly opposes the Spirit's

---

[56] John F. Walvoord, *The Holy Spirit* (Grand Rapids, MI: Zondervan Publishing House, 1958), 199.

control with intense temptation, enticement, and cunning persuasion to cause us to sin daily. The Spirit is not grieved by the presence of the sin nature, but by the sins we commit by not resisting its control. "Grieve not" is an exhortation to us to allow nothing into our lives that is contrary to the holiness of the Spirit. God has designed three provisions for meeting this condition.

The first provision is found in Romans 6:1–13 about accepting by faith the *crucifixion of our sin nature*. Our identification with Christ by Spirit baptism into Christ's death, burial and resurrection leads us to present ourselves to God, and to cease "presenting the members of our body to sin as instruments of unrighteousness; but present...your members as instruments of righteousness to God" (6:13). Paul alludes to the same doctrine when he says, "And do not be conformed [actually *"stop being conformed"*] to this world" (Rom. 12:2a), indicating that it is possible since Christ, through the Holy Spirit's control, is now our Master and we can choose not to serve sin. This is a preventive provision from God and when in spite of it we do sin, we can blame only ourselves. However, when we do sin, our loving and gracious God has designed a second provision.

We know that dedication settles the question of quenching the Spirit, because it settles the question of who is running our lives and the Spirit's direction and guidance in pursuing the will of God. But our growing sensitivity to the Spirit and His work in our lives may also reveal from time to time a lack of fellowship with God as He makes known the presence of some sin that we must deal with though confession. Admittedly we all sin, and the remedy for grieving the Spirit in this way is summed up in God's second provision with the word *confess*, as described by John when he writes, "If we confess our sins, He is faithful and righteous to forgive us our sins and to cleanse us from all unrighteousness" (1 John 1:9).

As we examine this provision, it is important to understand that this is presented by John as the basis for the *Christian's* fellowship with God (1 John 1:5—2:2). A careful reading of the entire passage reveals that the sins dealt with here are the believer's sins that break or disrupt our fellowship with God (not our relationship with God which was settled at conversion). In other words, though our relationship with God as His child is not broken by these sins, our fulfilling, joyous family fellowship with God and other believers is broken or disturbed. Notice also that our confession must come before restoration into fellowship is possible (1:9).

The word "confess" in this verse means to agree with God about these particular sins, to see them as He sees them, and admit that His assessment is correct. In our spiritual growth and maturing process, we may become aware of sins of which we were previously unaware, but He graciously points them out to us. The Spirit wants us to know about them and deal with them. Confession is a part of a healthy and growing relationship with God. As one writer says,

> Confession by its very nature is a sanctifying force. The Christian who has agonized before God in the knowledge of his own guilt and claimed the cleansing of the precious blood will by this very operation be less prone to return to the paths of sin.... The act of confession also in effect is an act of dependence upon

God, a recognition of human weakness and of the need of divine power. [57]

Known sin causes the Spirit to be grieved, fellowship disturbed, and useful service hindered. In response, God gives us time and opportunity for proper self-adjustment and confession of sin. However, if we neglect this opportunity and persist in our sin, our loving and gracious heavenly Father employs His third provision of *discipline*, designed to bring us back to confession. Discipline, often referred to as chastening, includes correction, punishment, training, and development. It is administered by our heavenly Father in love (Heb. 12:6) to correct the believer and restore a righteous relationship with us.

> but He disciplines us for our good, so that we may share His holiness. All discipline for the moment seems not to be joyful, but sorrowful; yet to those who have been trained by it, afterwards it yields the peaceful fruit of righteousness. (Heb. 12:10b–11)

Since God's disciplining covers the entire area of "child training" designed to produce such positive results we need to apply the principle: *We must accept and thank God for any and all discipline as an expression of His love that is for our good, so that we may share His holiness, and being trained by it yield the peaceful fruit of righteousness (Heb. 12:5, 10, 11).* Discipline can be both purifying, as He disciplines to rid us of impurities; and it can be preventive, as He disciplines us

---

[57] John F. Walvoord, *The Holy Spirit* (Grand Rapids, MI: Zondervan Publishing House, 1958), 202.

so we won't do it again. Discipline is not needed when we respond to newly identified sin with proper self-judgment and confession.

"Walk by the Spirit"

The third condition that must be met in order to be filled with the Holy Spirit is expressed with a positive command that clearly validates the principle: *We need to walk by the Spirit—relying upon the power and the indwelling presence of the Spirit to do for us, in us, and through us, what we cannot do for ourselves.* Paul declares "But I say, walk by the Spirit, and you will not carry out the desire of the flesh" (Gal. 5:16), for in reality the negative commands of quench not the Spirit and grieve not the Spirit would not be needed if the desires of the flesh were not expressed.

To *walk* by the Spirit means to *live by means of* or *in dependence upon the Holy Spirit.* It clearly identifies the Spirit-filled or Spirit-controlled life as a life of conscious dependence upon the Holy Spirit. In other words, it is walking by means of the power and the indwelling presence of the Spirit as He supplies His enablement to be expressed in and through us resulting in the accomplishment of God's will. We know that walking is an action, but the present tense of the verb emphasizes the continual nature of that experience. A literal translation would be, "continue or keep on walking in dependence upon the Spirit." Every parent and adult knows that walking is a skill that is developed over months and even years, and with the skill of walking in dependence on the Spirit comes a growing confidence that the Spirit can and will provide the support and enablement needed for godly living with contentment, which reinforces the principle: *As we experience walking in conscious dependence upon the Holy Spirit, we must keep on developing our skill and building our confidence in Him as He enables us to resist the relentless enemy of the flesh (Gal. 5:16).*

The necessity for walking in dependence upon the Spirit is evident as we consider the high standard of spiritual maturity for members of the body of Christ in whom He indwells. We are exhorted to love one another as Christ loves us (John 13:34; 15:12), and to "be longsuffering toward all," and "always follow after that which is good" (1 Thess. 5:14–15). We are commanded to "Rejoice always. Pray without ceasing. In everything give thanks" (1 Thess. 5:16–18). Multiplied examples of behavior impossible for the flesh could be included which prove that things impossible for man unassisted by the Spirit are possible for us when we are walking in dependence upon the Spirit (Gal. 5:16).

The challenge of attaining the high standard of maturity in Christ becomes even more difficult as we continually confront the present world system with its ungodly and corrupting influence. We are told that friendship with the world is spiritual adultery making us an enemy of God (Jas. 4:4). We are exhorted not to love the world nor the things in the world because this is the expression of the flesh, not the Spirit (1 John 2:15). Furthermore our warfare is essentially with Satan, and we are warned that the devil prowls like a roaring lion seeking to destroy our testimony (1 Pet. 5:5), and that only the full armor of God can make us able to stand firm against the schemes of the devil (Eph. 6:11).

By combining the high standard of spiritual maturity and the opposition by such powerful, strong, clever, and relentless enemies, our only option is to continually walk in dependence upon the Spirit, which in reality is letting the Spirit have full control. Now that's what the filling of the Spirit is all about: (a) once-for-all dedication of life in answer to quenching the Spirit; (b) victory over known sin through confession and restoration to fellowship in answer to grieving the Spirit; (c) and constant dependence upon the Spirit in response to walking by the Spirit. Therefore in principle: *We must remain sensitive to maintaining the three conditions for the filling of the Spirit for when they are being met the filling is automatically experienced and the fruit of the Spirit is unleashed to produce our growth, maturity and effective ministry in the body of Christ.* What a beautiful and powerful force this is for both the one who is filled and the Spirit who fills and controls. Notice also that it is "fruit" singular, not fruits, which means that all nine features are always present and they function in tandem as the Spirit directs and enables. The following explanation is insightful:

> Christian character is not mere moral or legal correctness, but the possession and the expression of nine graces: *love, joy, peace*—character as an inward state; *longsuffering, gentleness, goodness*—character in expression toward man; *faith, meekness, self-control*—character in expression toward God. Taken together they present a moral portrait of Christ, and may be taken as the apostle's explanation of Galatians 2:20, "not I but Christ.... This character is possible because of the believer's vital union to Christ (Jn. 15:5; 1 Cor.

12:12–13) and is wholly the fruit of the Spirit in those believers who are yielded to Him.[58]

We have learned much about what it means to walk by the Spirit and the victory over the flesh and the evil forces that meeting this condition guarantees (Gal. 5:16). A reading of this entire passage (Gal.5:16–26) clearly reveals that we are dealing with an internal conflict, especially when Paul says, "For the flesh sets its desire against the Spirit, and the Spirit against the flesh; for these are in opposition to one another, so that your may not do the things you please" (5:17).

It is important, however, to notice that Paul's description of the despicable, immoral, ungodly, and wicked desires of the flesh (5:19–21) begins with the words "Now the deeds of the flesh are evident" (5:19). The word "evident" is a strong term describing open or plain behavior that is practiced in a blatant and unashamed manner. This is another reminder that our thoughts control our attitudes and our attitudes control our actions, and any failure in this internal struggle will be openly displayed whenever we cease to maintain this gracious condition of walking by the Spirit. But on the bright side of the internal conflict is the Spirit's opportunity to accomplish His ultimate objective of our walk by the Spirit, and that is His glorious display of the fruit of the Spirit (5:22–26), which is Christ-likeness visible in and through our Spirit-enabled behavior.

The spectacular contrast of the fruit of the Spirit over the desires of the flesh can only be achieved supernaturally by God, yet it is the expression of God's heart for our rule of

---

[58] C. I. Scofield, *The Scofield Reference Bible* (New York, NY: Oxford University Press, 1945), 1247 (note on Galatians 5:22).

life provided by the death of Christ and walking by the Spirit. Paul explains, "Now those who belong to Christ Jesus have crucified the flesh with its passions and desires. Since we live by the Spirit, let us also walk by the Spirit" (5:24-25).

The Holy Spirit Teaches

On the night before the crucifixion, as Christ explained to the disciples the things that were about to happen to Him and to them, He assured them that in light of His beneficial departure, God the Father would be sending "another Helper," whom Christ identified as the "Spirit of truth," who would "be in them forever" (John 14:16–17). Then He added, "But the Helper, the Holy Spirit, whom the Father will send in My name, He will teach you all things, and bring to your remembrance all that I said to you" (14:26). It is very clear that Christ is introducing the Spirit's strategic ministry of teaching that would enhance and enrich all that Christ had been and would yet teach them before His ascension. Consider how this special teaching role is so characteristic of God the Spirit. It is the Holy Spirit who inspired the writers of the entire Bible (2 Tim. 3:16; 2 Pet. 1:20–21) and who now, by His permanent indwelling of every believer, is available to teach all things from that completed Bible, in order to fill, control, direct, and enable every member of the body of Christ who is willing to pursue godly living with commitment.

Christ expands the amazing details of this promise by saying,

> I have many more things to say to you, but you cannot bear them now. But when He, the Spirit of truth,

comes, He will guide you into all the truth; for He will not speak of on His own initiative, but whatever He hears, He will speak; and He will disclose to you what is to come. He will glorify Me, for He will take of Mine and will disclose it to you. All things that the Father has are Mine, therefore I said that He takes of Mine and will disclose it to you. (John 16:12–15)

When Christ spoke these words, this teaching ministry of the Holy Spirit through remembrance and revelation was future for all of the one hundred and twenty believers, including the disciples. But then on the day of Pentecost, Peter's sermon that displayed his amazing recollection and incredible comprehension of the truth, including numerous Old Testament quotes and truth Jesus had taught about His death, burial, resurrection, and ascension was convincing evidence that this promised teaching ministry had begun. It is important to point out that the Greek text specifies "all *the* truth" (16:13a), implying that all the things we now learn about Christ must come from the completed Bible, so the Spirit teaches us the content of Scripture that includes "what is to come" or prophecy (16:13b). Take note also that the Spirit does not teach His own message, but what He hears from the Lord Jesus Christ. That which He discloses will glorify Christ as the body of Christ is edified and built up. Furthermore, whenever the Word of God is taught in the power of the Spirit, Christ will be glorified.

Without question, Paul is one of the most prominent examples of the Holy Spirit's teaching ministry both in (1) receiving the major portion of new revelation, prophetic interpretation, and doctrinal clarification for founding and establishing the church and (2) exercising the Spiritual gift of teaching through speaking, writing, an exemplary life-style, as well as an evangelistic missionary and church planting work. The Spirit directed Paul to write a lengthy passage (1 Cor. 2:9—3:3) telling us how it is possible to understand the deep things of God by saying,

> The things which eye has not seen and ear has not heard, and which have not entered the heart of man, all that God has prepared for those who love Him. For to us God has revealed them through the Spirit for the Spirit searches all things, even the depths of God. (1 Cor. 2:9–10)

He then stresses the Spirit's teaching when he says, "Now we have received not the spirit of the world, but the Spirit who is from God, so that we may know the things freely given to us by God" (2:12). One writer, in discussing the context of this passage focuses on the qualifications for being taught these deep things by the Spirit and the consequences for failing to meet them when he writes,

> it is made clear that the deeper things of spiritual truth can only be understood by those who are spiritually qualified to be taught by the Spirit. The natural man is unable to understand even the simple truths understood by those who are Spirit-taught. The appalling ignorance of many Christians concerning the things of the Word of God is directly traceable to

their carnality (vs. 3:1-3) and failure in seeking the blessings of a life filled with the Spirit.[59]

Christ's teaching (John 16:12-15) and Paul's presentation (1 Cor. 2:9—3:3) delineate for us the principle: *Failure to meet or maintain the conditions for the filling of the Spirit precludes us from understanding or progressing in the deep things of God (1 Cor. 2:10, 12-13, 15-16; 3:1-2).* Ironically, after the entire congregation had been commended in Chapter 1 for their positive spiritual life and testimony (1:1-9), and were then taught in Chapter 2 about understanding and progressing in the deep things of God (2:9-16), Paul, in Chapter 3 identified as carnal (3:1-2). This resulted in a portion of that same congregation, when faced with a difficult issue, failed to walk by the Spirit, and the flesh prevailed as Paul describes in Gal. 5:16-17, "so that you may not do the things that you please" (5:17). We have learned that this is correctable by confessing and being restored to walking by the Spirit. No matter how far we may have strayed from walking by the Spirit, it is never too late to pursue and employ preventive measures as described by a popular bible scholar and writer:

> Every Christian needs to have a sound, true biblical understanding of God and His truth, *and we must never stop growing in our pursuit of that goal.* The writer of Hebrews chided his readers because they had stalled at the very basics. "You have become dull of hearing" he told them in Hebrews 5:11. They needed to reboot, to start learning and growing again—not only for their

---

[59] John F. Walvoord, *The Holy Spirit* (Grand Rapids, MI: Zondervan Publishing House, 1958), 220-21.

own sakes, but because it is every Christian's duty to be a discipler of others.... They needed to move beyond simple basics and gain a grown-up understanding of the Christian faith.... Their spiritual growth had been stunted by their own apathy, inattention, lethargy, or whatever. Now they could not comprehend the more substantial truths they desperately needed to learn, because "solid food is for the mature, for those who have their powers of discernment trained by constant practice to distinguish good from evil." (v. 14 English Standard Version)[60]

The Holy Spirit Leads

The Holy Spirit's ministry of leading has a particularly close relationship to His ministry of teaching since both are vitally important elements in our Christian experience and both are essential in our continual pursuit of the will of God. While the Spirit's teaching is aimed at providing us with a clear understanding of the content of the Word of God, the leading of the Spirit deals specifically with the application of that biblical content in determining God's will in any given situation. When Paul comments, "For all who are being led by the Spirit of God, these are the sons of God" (Rom. 8:14), he uses the term "sons of God" instead of "children." This identifies them not only as Christians, but as spiritually mature, Spirit-filled Christians who not only continually access the Spirit's teaching but they consistently apply that

---

[60] John MacArthur, "Forward" in Paul Enns, *The Moody Handbook of Theology,* Revised and Expanded Edition (Chicago, IL: Moody Press, 2008), 13.

truth as they access the Spirit's leading for God's will in their day-to-day experiences.

God's leading may even vary in similar instances due to such things as identifiable or unknown circumstances, hindrances, or timing factors, thereby stressing our need for every detail of each instance to be discussed with God. We can pray with confidence that the Holy Spirit can and will reveal both the answer and the identification of specific timing needed to fulfill the perfect will of God. These details provide the basis for the principle: *When we let ourselves continually be filled [controlled] with the Holy Spirit, God's leading becomes our personal, intimate, and privileged source of guidance for our life in the center of God's will (Rom. 8:14).*

The Holy Spirit Prays

As Christians who determine to pursue godly living with contentment, we often need encouragement and hope to deal with our overwhelming challenges while "waiting eagerly for our adoption as sons, the redemption of our body" (Rom. 8:23). We can find that encouragement and hope as Paul brings us a word of hope in the uplifting truth that the Holy Spirit in us is praying for us according to the will of God,

> In the same way the Spirit also helps our weakness, for we do not know how to pray as we should, but the Spirit Himself intercedes for us with groanings too deep for words; and He who searches the hearts knows what the mind of the Spirit is, because He intercedes for the saints according to the will of God. (Rom. 8:26–27)

Notice that the word "weakness" (8:26) is singular because it relates to our total need for dependence upon the Spirit in every area, but in the immediate context it relates particularly to our weakness in knowing what to pray for at a given moment. The word "helps" pictures someone helping another carry a heavy load as the Spirit comes to the rescue and literally "keeps on interceding for us with groans that words cannot express" (8:26) while assuring us that "...He intercedes for the saints according to the will of God" (8:27b). One writer adds, "In another passage we are told that the Spirit guides and directs our prayers (Eph. 6:18). This is more the guidance of the believer's heart and mind as he prays than the unutterable groanings of the Spirit Himself."[61] He then concludes his discussion of the Spirit's praying ministry with,

> The result of such a prayer life is assurance to the believer of the certainty of his future and full redemption (Rom. 8:23). This ministry of the Spirit is a kind of earnest-like guarantee of that redemption. Such a satisfying prayer life will help keep us content in this present world as we wait for the consummation. The ministry of the Spirit, then, is not only connected with answered prayer, but it cultivates our assurance and contentment in this life.[62]

---

[61] Charles C. Ryrie, *Basic Theology* (Chicago, IL: Moody Press, 1999), 382.
[62] *Ibid.*

Summary and Review of Stewardship of Talents/Abilities

To become a Christian in the U.S. is undoubtedly a very significant and meaningful personal event. Yet few of us faced any outward opposition or hostility by making this important decision to accept Christ as our Savior and receive eternal life. In all probability, it was a relatively small circle of people who knew or even seemed to care when we made our second most important decision by presenting our body to God as a living sacrifice. This resulted in steps of spiritual growth, enhanced by seriously studying the Bible and fellowshipping with other believers. This involved total dedication to God and doing His will for the remainder of our earthly life. This qualified us to pursue godly living with contentment. It also gave us confidence that moment by moment we can maturely serve God in whatever way the Spirit leads with all of the abilities, spiritual gifts, and enablement He provides for fulfilling our trustworthy stewardship of talents and abilities.

Perhaps, a brief review of one most biblically documented examples will give us increasing clarity regarding the process and see how it matches our own experience. This process is responsible for opening the potential for godly living with contentment and the trustworthy stewardship of our talents and abilities. The example is none other than Saul of Tarsus whom we know better as the Apostle Paul, and the record of his conversion and transformation is basically found in three passages in the book of Acts (9:1–18; 22:1-16; 26:9–18).

The setting for Paul's conversion is aptly described with these words:

> No conversion is more significant in all the New Testament then that of Saul of Tarsus, the archenemy of Christians in the first century. Had a list been made of those least likely ever to humble themselves before the Lord Jesus Christ, Saul would have appeared *first* on the list, without question. But God (who has never met His match!) took hold of Saul's life and turned him around full circle. The persecutor became a preacher of the gospel, the greatest missionary in all of time, and the most prolific writer in the Bible.[63]

The account of Saul's vicious persecution is familiar to most of us. We see his zealous desire to intensify his efforts as the text describes:

> Now Saul, still breathing threats and murder against the disciples of the Lord, went to the high priest [in Jerusalem] and asked for letters from him to the synagogues at Damascus, so that if he found any belonging to the Way, both men and women, he might bring them bound to Jerusalem. (9:1–2)

It was during his travel from Jerusalem to Damascus that God intervened with different plans for Saul and *two things* occurred in this encounter that define his process. Notice that the encounter included a combination of the blinding

---

[63] Charles R. Swindoll, *Bible Study Guide* (Fullerton, CA: Insights for Living, 1979), 72.

light from heaven at noontime that was brighter than the sun, (22:6; 26:13) and a voice saying, "Saul, Saul, why are you persecuting me?" (9:4). When Saul responded with, "Who are You, Lord?" (9:5a), it was beginning to dawn on Saul that Jesus, whose claims he had declared were blasphemy and whose resurrection he denied, was the Messiah and Lord. This is supported by Saul's use of the word "Lord," which means Master (one to whom service is due). Then when the Lord said, "I am Jesus whom you are persecuting," (9:5b), the life-changing truth Saul had perceived was confirmed. By recognizing Jesus as the true Messiah and placing his faith in Him, Paul immediately became a new man in Christ, and that's the *first thing* that resulted from the encounter.

Now someone might suggest that Saul accepted Christ because God convinced him with a spectacular and supernatural event—one in which most would respond in the same way. However, we have already seen that the Holy Spirit convicted and convinced us in a spectacular and supernatural way, enabling us to accept Christ when we were dead in sin and not seeking after God.

No one would deny that Paul was a strong-willed individual both before and after his conversion and that trait resulted in his strong commitment to the things he believed to be true. Consequently, no sooner had he settled the issue of his salvation, he settled the matter of yielding to God and His will in dedication (Rom. 12:1–2) by asking the question "What shall I do?" (Acts 22:10). In other words, the *second thing* this encounter accomplished was that Paul offered the Lord all of his life for service without reservation.

As Paul so impressively allowed himself to be launched totally into a life of fruitful ministry and service that vividly displayed godly living with contentment while fulfilling in a trustworthy manner his stewardship of talents and abilities, we will conclude our study of the subject with the words of Paul written about this very encounter some 30 years later to young Timothy:

> I thank Christ Jesus our Lord, who has strengthened me, because He considered me faithful, putting me into service, even though I was formerly a blasphemer and a persecutor and a violent aggressor. Yet I was shown mercy because I acted ignorantly in unbelief; and the grace of our Lord was more than abundant, with the faith and love which are found in Christ Jesus. It is a trustworthy statement, deserving full acceptance, that Christ Jesus came into the world to save sinners, among whom I am foremost of all. Yet for this reason, I found mercy, so that in me as the foremost, Jesus Christ might demonstrate His perfect patience as an example for those who would believe in Him for eternal life. Now to the King eternal, immortal, invisible, the only God, be honor and glory forever and ever. Amen. (1 Tim. 1:12–17)

Principles from Holy Spirit's Work in Salvation

Convicting Work of the Spirit—that with every bit of talent, ability, and enablement the Spirit provides, we must zealously engage in our sole responsibility to (1) clearly and accurately communicate the gospel with our lips, (2) consistently display its presence in our daily activities, and (3) continually pray that the Holy Spirit will be pleased to use it to convict and convince the unsaved to accept Christ (John 16:7–11, p. 124).

Regenerating Work of the Spirit—the purpose of God's making us new creatures is so that believers will do good works (Eph. 2:10, p. 126).

Indwelling Work of the Spirit—since our bodies are the temple of the Holy Spirit, we should be motivated to glorify God with our body through moral purity (1 Cor. 6:19–20, p. 129). The Foundational Principle of Spiritual Enablement—godly stewardship of material resources, talents, and time can only be accomplished by depending upon the Holy Spirit to do in us, for us, and through us, what we cannot do in our own strength (John 14:16–17, p. 129).

Baptizing Work of the Spirit (Foundational Principle of Balance)—God's balanced design for the body of Christ with its many members, provides great potential for Christ's church to declare the excellencies of God to the world as it reveals the perfect balance between unity, diversity, and interdependence (Rom. 12:1–2, p. 131).

Sealing Work of the Spirit—our sensitivity to the *Person* of the Holy Spirit, God's seal of ownership, should motivate us to employ every benefit He has provided, while completely depending upon His direction in order to keep from grieving Him by sinning (Eph. 4:30, p. 133).

Principles from Holy Spirit's Work in the Christian's Daily Life

The Holy Spirit Gives Spiritual Gifts—God has endowed us with God-given spiritual abilities, God-given natural abilities, and God-given acquired abilities to be used for building up the body of Christ through the Spirit's directing and enabling our trustworthy stewardship of those abilities (p. 138). As we positively respond to the Spirit's direction by taking every opportunity He provides to exercise the gifts He has given, we should do it zealously and with complete confidence that we are functioning as God's servants fulfilling God's purpose of building up the body of Christ in the right place at the right time (p. 140).

The Filling of the Holy Spirit—our yielding to the will of God is a matter of accepting it as the rule of life by electing it to be final even before we know what He may wish us to do, which means being willing to do anything (Rom. 12:1; 6:13, p. 147). We must accept and thank God for any and all discipline as an expression of His love that is for our good, so that we may share His holiness, and being trained by it yield the peaceful fruit of righteousness (Heb. 12:5, 10, 11, p. 83). When we let ourselves continually be filled (controlled) with the Holy Spirit, God's leading becomes our personal, intimate, and privileged source of guidance for our life in the center of God's will (Rom. 8:14, p. 151).

CHAPTER 9

Stewardship of Time:
How to invest the time
given to us by God

Distribution and Responsibility

The stewardship of material resources and the stewardship of talents and abilities both have basic similarities that distinguish them from the stewardship of time. Whether it's material resources or talents and abilities, God's distribution differs from one believer to another, but time is equally distributed to all of us even if it is a day, a week, a month, or a year. And when we are dealing with material resources or talents and abilities, we must make stewardship choices related to the will of God such as whether to use or not use, to spend or keep, to respond or to ignore. But the stewardship of time is different. No matter how much we would like to be able to adjust the passing of time, we cannot slow or stop the clock or cause it to speed up. Nor can we buy time or give it away. We have all the time we need, but that never seems to be enough.

At the end of an hour, we have all had sixty minutes—a precious portion of our life—that can never be reclaimed.

It's important to realize that we already know the will of God regarding the twenty-four hour day for His entire creation. It was determined on the first day of creation as described: "God called the light day, and the darkness He called night. And there was evening and there was morning, one day." In so doing God predetermined that human beings (created on the sixth day, Gen. 1:26–31) would have the time spent that belongs to Him and He entrusted to us; one day at a time consisting of twenty-four hours, no more and no less. The most important question we have to address in the stewardship of time is: Does time manage us, or do we let God enable us to become trustworthy stewards (managers) of our time by "making the most of our time" which literally means "redeeming the time" (Eph. 5:16a)? The goal for us is not to *find more time,* but to use our time wisely. This is the one element we can change. When writing to the spiritually mature Ephesian church, Paul gives this relevant advice that can be appropriately applied by any Christian as an antidote to the problem we all continually face:

> Look carefully then how you walk! Live purposefully and worthily and accurately, not as the unwise and witless, but as wise—sensible, intelligent people; Making the very most of the time—buying up each opportunity—because the days are evil. Therefore do not be vague and thoughtless and foolish, but understanding and firmly grasping what the will of the Lord is. (Eph. 5:15–17 TLB)

Notice carefully that the first direction Paul gives is a call for wisdom (5:15). Therefore, we must recall what James says, "if any of you lacks wisdom, let him ask of God, who gives to all generously...and it will be given to him" (Jas. 1:5). The need for wisdom is even further supported by Paul's command to "be filled with the Spirit" (Eph. 5:18). Additionally, don't miss the stress for urgency that loudly echoes the challenges we face daily in our current American culture—"because the days are evil" (Eph. 5:16b).

It's not difficult to realize that in capitalistic, corporate America there would be an abundance of excellent time management programs. Fortunately, some of the most effective have been designed by Christians. We recommend one author who writes:

> Much is said regarding the stewardship of wealth and possessions. Less is said about stewardship of talent. Little is said concerning stewardship of time. Perhaps even less is understood. What do we mean by being 'stewards of time'? Is it really our time we're talking about, or is it God's time? Has it been granted to us, along with the gift of life itself, to be disposed according to our own purposes...with only a portion of our own determining going back to Him from whence it came?... Management of time thus becomes for the Christian, management of His time. And this brings us to what may appear to be a slightly revolutionary thought. When times get out of joint...when tasks pile up...and when things go wrong...how often do we stop and ask God if we're doing what *He* want us to do? It is His time we're managing, isn't this where we should begin?[64]

---

[64] Ted W. Engstrom and R. Alec Mackenzie, *Managing Your Time* (Grand Rapids, MI: Zondervan, 1967), 24.

Another writer suggests:

> since God fashioned the world and all that is in it, does all our time belong to Him?... A truly effective life does not result from getting God to help us. Our lives assume maximum worth when we turn our wills over to Him and ask that we might be of assistance to His purposes.[65]

By giving each of us twenty-four hours of His time daily that is being irrecoverably spent according to His creative design (Gen.1:5—2:3; Ex. 20:8–11) without an available choice not to spend it, God has framed two principles: *Our individual trustworthy stewardship of time means our responsibility is to manage twenty-four hours of God's time each day with wisdom that enables us to redeem the time in keeping with His will for us (Eph. 5:15–17)* and *our individual trustworthy stewardship of time responsibility is to be applied with a sense of urgency because the days are evil (Eph. 5:16b).*

Recognition of God's *equal distribution* of time throughout our life, together with our inescapable stewardship of time responsibility, provides sufficient motivation for our trustworthy response in time management that will indeed represent "making the most of our time" (Eph. 5:16a). Any added motivational thrust to begin or sustain effective time management could well be provided by Paul's comment about glorifying God in both life and death when he says:

> Therefore, we also have as our ambition, whether at home or absent, to be pleasing to Him. For we must all

---

[65] Charlie W. Shedd, *Time for All Things* (Nashville, TN: Abingdon, 1980), 14.

appear before the judgment seat of Christ, so that each one may be recompensed for his deeds in the flesh, according to what he has done, whether good or bad. (2 Cor. 5:9–10)

Brevity of Human Life

Paul's focus on wisdom needed to make the most of our time and to determine what the will of the Lord is (Eph. 5:15–17) requires that we clearly understand the biblical concept of brevity, or as the dictionary defines it, "the shortness of time."

The brevity of human life is definitively addressed by God through a prayer of Moses in Psalm 90 that provides great insight regarding our trustworthy stewardship of time. The prayer begins by describing our omnipotent, eternal God who is not subject to time:

Lord, through all generations you have been our home! Before the mountains were created, before the earth was formed, you are God without beginning or end. You speak, and man turns back to dust. A thousand years are but as yesterday to you! They are like a single hour!" (Ps. 90:1-4, TLB)

In contrast, Moses then describes the brevity of life:

We glide along the tides of time as swiftly as a racing river, and vanish as quickly as a dream. We are like grass that is green in the morning but mowed down and withered before the evening shadows fall....

Seventy years are given us! And some may even live to eighty." (Ps. 90:5-6, 10a, TLB)

No matter how many or few days of our brief life we may yet have and in light of the certainty of death, the wisdom of God is expressed as Moses prays, "Teach us to number our days and recognize how few they are; *help us to spend them as we should*" (Ps. 90:12, TLB, emphasis added).

While the brevity of life emphasizes the importance of our careful, trustworthy stewardship of time, it seems reasonable to believe that since God has promised to "supply all our needs according to His riches in glory in Christ Jesus" (Phil. 4:19), He will provide all the time needed for Him to accomplish in and through us all He desires. God gives us, even as He gave His Son, sufficient time each day for us to fulfill His perfect plan—including interruptions. Our best response then begins immediately by exercising the disciplined, trustworthy stewardship of our time, combined with our commitment to godliness with contentment, a firm desire to become what God wants us to become, while agreeing with David, "But as for me, I trust in Thee, O Lord, I say, 'Thou art my God.' My times are in Thy hand...." (Ps. 31:13–15a). This response is especially appropriate since the schedule for the end of our earthly life, like the schedule for the Rapture of the church, the body of Christ, are both totally in God's hands and unknown to us, thus motivating us to live each day as the last in which we can glorify Him.

Distractions

In order for us to be "making the most of our time" (Eph. 5:16b) Paul not only focuses on wisdom, but he gives warnings that help us identify sources that produce distractions. With his *first* warning he said "walk, not as unwise men" (5:15b) in contrast to "wise." This is clearly a reference to the wisdom of the natural or carnal man (both of whom are controlled by the flesh) in contrast to the spiritual man (who is controlled by the Spirit) and who is able to assess or discern all things as the Spirit directs (1 Cor. 2:6—3:3). The *second* warning, "because the days are evil" (5:16b), obviously applies to our affluent, worldly American culture. As you know, since our culture continually entices us to ungodly, unwise, unnecessary, and useless expenditures of time, we really need spiritual discernment in our time management. *Finally*, Paul warns us against being "foolish" in contrast to "understanding what the will of the Lord is" (5:17). This foolishness refers to such things as procrastination, laziness or time wasted in things that may not be evil in themselves, but are unnecessary and nonessential activities, at the expense of effort invested in knowing and doing the "good, acceptable and perfect will of God" (Rom. 12:2).

Most of us are very much aware that retirement, with abundant financial resources and benefits is perhaps the most common and acceptably sought after goal in our affluent American culture. It is considered adequate when it enables the recipient to enjoy at least the following—no responsibility, no accountability, no required productivity, a sizable home (usually larger than needed) or even two or more houses for personal use, one or more new or newer cars, income to cover all expenses (including insurance, maintenance, and pleasure trips i.e. cruises, tours, etc.), plus invested funds available to cover any possible emergency, and finally twenty-four hours of God's time every day that is to be used in whatever way we choose, but generally for self-gratification.

For decades retirement has been considered an honorable objective to achieve for anyone, including Christians. And we must hasten to add that there is nothing improper for a Christian to accept what he or she has appropriately earned. It is plain to see that such a retirement package touches every area of our Christian stewardship but because of the pervasive influences of our secular culture, some potential distractions can subtly be presented for which we must seek the Spirit's direction regarding our involvement. While at the same time, a number of positive examples should be considered by Christian retirees. For instance, think of the positive benefit that might be derived from acquired time that was unavailable before retirement. It is realistic that a tremendous pool of retired volunteers could be unleashed immediately to provide incredible numbers of productive hours for all kinds of service and ministry. Some retirees are already engaged in this kind of trustworthy stewardship of time effort, but we know that so much more is available and the possibilities are almost unlimited.

In order to assist us in the process of considering such retirement issues, we need to remember at least the following elements of retirement in order to make effective Spirit directed evaluations and adjustments.

- The first reality is that retirement as designed by the secular culture is aimed at satisfying personal gratification rather than God's glorification. Consequently, Spirit-led evaluation and adjustment from that perspective is absolutely essential.

- The second reality that may be unknown to many is that no concept of retirement is taught or even suggested in the New Testament as God's intended goal or objective for members of the body of Christ, the Church. In fact, God's provisions and enablement for spiritual growth, maturity, service in trustworthy stewardship, and godly living, are designed to be applied in response to the retirement culture in the same way they are to be applied to any positive or negative cultural issue. In other words, when secular culture conflicts, distorts, or opposes our understanding of and conformity to the will of God, the precepts, principles, adaptations, and adjustments remain in place for us to apply. We must not allow the secular ungodly culture to change, confuse, or distort our commitment to knowing and doing the will of God for the remainder of our earthly life.

- The third reality is that retirement can and should be the most dynamic and significant spiritually uplifting lifestyle change we could ever encounter. On one hand, the required time (forty to sixty hours per week), talents and abilities (physical, mental, relational etc.), and material resources (expenses and investments), are no longer required for providing our basic essential needs and related discretionary purposes. Such dramatic changes free up incredible amounts of time, talents and abilities, plus material resources for each retiree's stewardship reallocation. The result on the other hand, is that God's faithful provisions and the Spirit's direction can be accessed for wisdom and guidance in making the required adjustments in our day-to-day lifestyle. This opens up the exciting process of selecting stewardship ministry and service opportunities to fill the time, talent and ability, and material resources made available by our retirement. In this way we expand our ministry and service stewardship in keeping with our previous continuing pursuit of godly living with contentment in order to fulfill trustworthy stewardship. Furthermore, by so doing, retirement that could easily be designed to satisfy personal gratification becomes retirement as an instrument God can employ to glorify Himself and richly bless us as we continue to become what He wants us to become.

The Plan

As we have addressed the stewardship of time, our intention has been to describe and explain the necessity for all of us to identify and use an effective time management plan or program. We trust that has been accomplished and you plan to continue with one you've already used and like or to look for another. Whatever your decision, make certain you don't fall into the trap indicated in the familiar cliché, "When we fail to plan, we are planning to fail," especially since many plans are quite easily obtainable and relatively simple to adapt for use. Though we have not yet made any specific recommendations, there is one extremely successful plan you may want to try after reading the very well known true story that describes it.

Over sixty-five years ago Bethlehem Steel president Charles Schwab approached management consultant Ivy Lee with an unusual challenge. "Show me a way to get more things done in my available time, and if it works, I'll pay anything within reason." Lee told him that it would be no problem and handed Schwab a piece of paper. "Write down the things you have to do tomorrow," he said. Schwab did it. "Now number these items in the order of their real importance," Lee continued. Schwab did that. "The first thing tomorrow morning," Lee said, "start working on number one and stay with it until it is completed. Then move on to number two and work on it until it's completed and so on through the day. If any task takes all day, stick with it as long as it's the most important one. The secret is to do this daily. Evaluate the relative importance of the things you have to get done; establish your priorities; record your plan of action; and stick to it. Do this every working day and after you have convinced yourself of the value of this system, have your personnel down the line try it. Test it as long as you like. Then send me a check for whatever you think the idea is worth."

Some weeks later Lee's mail contained a $25,000.00 check from Schwab, who went on to build Bethlehem Steel into the globe's biggest independent steel company and to do it within five years. "Lee's advice," Schwab said, "was the single most valuable investment made by Bethlehem that year."

The plan described and applied in this very successful experience is one that originated in the mind of men totally immersed in the world system who, as far as we can determine, functioned apart from any real spiritual relationship with God or Spirit direction. However, it appears that this plan, applied with adequate spiritual wisdom and discernment, could be beneficially employed by godly individuals or organizations.

No matter what time management plan we select and employ, we must not forget the great challenges that still remain. The first challenge is to intentionally avoid the distractions that can so easily confuse, distort and damage our progress. Since *Webster* defines time as "the period during which action or process occur," the stewardship of time interconnects all three stewardships. Therefore the second, and perhaps the greater challenge means that our trustworthy stewardship of time ultimately enables us to fulfill our trustworthy stewardship of material resources, as well as our stewardship of talents and abilities in becoming what God wants us to become for Him and His glory.

There is one event on God's calendar that we must focus on again before we conclude the discussion of our stewardship of His time. That event is the return of the Lord Jesus Christ for us. In the New Testament alone, activities related to the return of Christ are alluded to numerous times. It is no wonder Paul tells Titus that we ought to be "Looking for the blessed hope and the appearing of the glory of our great God and Savior, Christ Jesus," and then motivates him with "who gave Himself for us to redeem us from every lawless deed, and to purify for Himself a people for His own possession, zealous for good deeds" (Tit. 2:13–14).

There are many similar passages filled with encouragement and promises related to Christ's return. We are assured that our commitment to the truth of His return enables us to "be steadfast, immovable, always abounding in the work of the Lord, knowing that our toil is not in vain in the Lord" (1 Cor. 15:51–58). To share the truth of the Rapture also provides a means of "comforting one another,...encouraging one another and building up one another" (1 Thess. 4:13–18; 5:1–11) and "having this hope *fixed* on Him purifies us, just as He is pure" (1 John 3:2).

The unique feature of this event is its scheduled timing, predetermined and known *only by God the Father*. Many other future events are precisely timed, such as the Tribulation, millennium, and the great white throne judgment, but their timing is actually dependent upon the trigger event, which of course is the Rapture, the removal of the body of Christ to be with Him forever. God has clearly indicated that "our blessed hope" could take place at any moment, even before you finish reading this page (Tit. 2:13). God has also confirmed that "For yet in a very little while He who is coming will come, and will not delay,... [*and while we are waiting*] My righteous ones shall live by faith" (Heb. 10:37–38a). So we know for certain He's coming and He will arrive right on schedule.

To express it succinctly, God's twofold intention is (1) to have us live and function every day for His glory as though it is our last day, giving us a sense of focus, commitment, urgency and desire for excellence in godliness with contentment. We are to be trustworthy stewards in every area as we continue to become what He wants us to become. At the same time, God desires us (2) to diligently pursue those same goals as though His return will not occur for an unknown period of days, months or even years, and do so with greater effectiveness, ministering grace and love seasoned with salt and shining with light both to the body of Christ and the lost world while daily anticipating His return.

By purposely designing Christ's sure return without revealing its scheduled time to us, God has framed two principles: *Excellence in the pursuit of godly living with contentment, in exercising trustworthy stewardship in every area, and our desire to become what God wants us to become should be our daily goal since this could be our last day to glorify God before the return of Christ (Heb. 10:37).* Second, *our objective must be to consistently grow in every area of our personal ministry and service so as to increase its impact in the body of Christ and the world since Christ may not return for years, even though we daily anticipate the blessed hope (Tit. 2:13–14).*

In the book of Ephesians Paul describes "ministry as the work of the saints to the building up of the body of Christ; until we all attain to the unity of the faith, and of the knowledge of the Son of God, to a mature man, to the measure of the stature which belongs to the fullness of Christ" (4:12b-13). In reality, that's what this book is all about. We have been continually urging the pursuit of godly living with contentment while engaging in trustworthy stewardship and sharpening our focus on becoming what God wants us to become for His glory. And since we are well aware that most, if not all of us usually need significant support and encouragement for maintaining these achievable objectives at an acceptable level, we want to share a list of ten statements about ministry we recently discovered. The list essentially covers every basic aspect of worship and provides an excellent profile for assessing our effectiveness of a genuine ministry life-style. The list should be read carefully, slowly, and thoughtfully. In fact, if we committed it to memory and reviewed it once a month until Christ returns, we should have little difficulty keeping our ministry on track. Here is the list and may God be glorified as we employ this excellent tool.

1. The foundation of ministry is character.
2. The nature of ministry is service.

3. The motive for ministry is love.
4. The measure of ministry is sacrifice.
5. The authority of ministry is submission.
6. The purpose of ministry is the glory of God.
7. The tools of ministry are the Word of God and prayer.
8. The privilege of ministry is growth.
9. The power of ministry is the Holy Spirit.
10. The model for ministry is Jesus Christ.[66]

Principles from the Stewardship of Time

Our individual trustworthy stewardship of time responsibility is to manage 24 hours of God's time each day with wisdom that enables us to redeem the time in keeping with His will for us (Eph. 5:15–17, p. 172).

Our individual trustworthy stewardship of time responsibility is to be applied with a sense of urgency because the days are evil (Eph. 5:16b, p. 172).

Excellence in the pursuit of godly living with contentment, in exercising trustworthy stewardship in every area, and our desire to become what God wants us to become should be our daily goal since this could be our last day to glorify God before the return of Christ, (Heb. 10:37, pp. 181-82).

Our objective must be to consistently grow in every area of our ministry so as to increase its impact in the body of Christ and the world since Christ may not return for years, even though we daily anticipate the blessed hope (Tit. 2:13–14, p. 182).

---

[66] Warren and David Wiersbe, *Making Sense of the Ministry* (Grand Rapids: Baker Books, 1983), 31-46, as cited in Charles R. Swindoll, *Rise and Shine: A Wake-up Call* (Portland, OR: Multinomah, 1989), 41.

CHAPTER 10

Stewardship of Life:
A perfect game plan for our journey

2 Peter 1:1–11 provides a perfect game plan for the journey that lies before us as we continue our on-going pursuit of godliness with contentment in order to become what God wants us to become in fulfilling our trustworthy stewardship. It's important to be reminded that our journey began with saving faith, even as Peter writes, "to those who have received a faith of the same kind as ours, by the righteousness of our God and Savior, Jesus Christ" (1:1). The Book of First Peter, as well as the following discussion, is directed toward those who believe that Jesus Christ, God's Son, died in their place for their sins and rose again (1 Cor. 15:1–11). Jesus Himself referred to this when He said, "For God so loved the world that He gave His only begotten Son, that whosoever believes in Him should not perish but have everlasting life" (John 3:16). As a result, the clear teaching of the Bible is that it is impossible for a person who is not a Christian, (1) to experience godly living or (2) to understand or possess true contentment.

The passage continues by teaching that the believer's life can be wholly transformed by a "knowledge" of God's

Word (2 Pet. 1:2, 3, 5, 6, 8). Indeed, this full knowledge is the means of experiencing a deep, personal relationship with God. Verse 3 states, "seeing that His divine power has granted to us everything pertaining to life and godliness, through the true knowledge of Him who called us by His own glory and excellence." Thus, *everything* we need for life and godliness comes through knowledge of Christ attained by faith in His Word (see also 1:4).

A vibrant faith in God, manifested by faith in His Word and an ever deepening relationship with Him, is then enriched and cultivated by "applying all diligence" (1:5), making every effort to develop the following qualities (1:5–7).

Moral Excellence—growth in faith begins by desiring to be like God Himself (the same word is used of God in 1:3). Morally upright in character through obedience to God's word, our faith does that which it is supposed to do with *excellence*.

Knowledge—the ability to discern God's will and orient one's life in accordance with that will. Faith is not distracted by ignorance, but rather possesses a practical knowledge that discerns between right and wrong when facing the duties of life so as to handle life successfully.

Self Control—faith possesses disciplined moderation. It controls one's own desires and cravings in keeping with knowledge in order to pursue God's will.

Perseverance—faith demonstrates inner endurance when circumstances are difficult. It faces the pressures of life without giving up or giving in to those pressures.

Godliness—faith seeks to please God in all things. Our behavior reflects the character of God and our lives are motivated by a desire to please Him.

Brotherly Kindness—faith demonstrates thoughtful, fervent, and practical consideration for other believers that then expresses itself in sensitive and meaningful action.

Love—faith is characterized by intelligent action that purposefully desires the highest good for the one being loved. It sacrifices itself to provide that which is morally excellent and beneficial.

The amazing and incredible consequences of possessing and increasing in these qualities as a consistent part of our character, is that we are guaranteed to be neither "useless" nor "unfruitful" in our productivity for Christ's glory (1:8). Furthermore, as long as we practice these things, we "will never stumble" (1:10). Meaning that whether material resources, talents and abilities, or time, the life-transforming knowledge of God attained through His Word by the power of the Holy Spirit makes our "calling and choosing by God" clearly evident (1:10) and assures us of a rich welcome into Christ's future kingdom—a wonderful welcome home, and "well done" by our Lord Himself (1:11; cf. Luke 19:17). Since there is no better way to live and conclude our earthly eternal life journey, we join with Peter in the spirit and nature of his reminders of "these things you already know, and have been established in the truth which is present with you" (1:12–15).

APPENDIX A

Tithing

The following is reproduced from Dr. Charles Caldwell Ryrie's book, *Balancing the Christian Life.*

But some will say, why go to all this trouble? Why not just take a tithe out of every paycheck and place it in the collection plate the following Sunday? The word *tithe* is found in the New Testament only eight times (Matt. 23:23; Luke 11:42; 18:12; Heb. 7:5–6, 8–9). In the references in the Gospels it is used in connection with that which the Pharisees were doing in fulfilling their obligation to the Mosaic law. In the references in Hebrews tithing is used to prove the inferiority of the Levitical priesthood to the Melchizedek priesthood. Since Levi paid tithes in Abraham when Abraham met Melchizedek, he demonstrates the recognized superiority of Melchizedek and of his priesthood. The passage does not go on and say (as is often implied) that we Christians, therefore, should pay tithes to Christ our High Priest.

It is apparent that the tithe was part of the Mosaic law (Lev. 27:30–33) and an important factor in the economy of Israel. The law was never given to Gentiles and is expressly done away for the Christian (Rom. 2:14; II Cor. 3:7–13; Heb. 7:11–12). Neither are the words of Malachi 3 for the Christian, for what believer claims to be a son of Jacob to whom the passage is addressed (v. 6)? Furthermore, material blessing is never promised today as an automatic reward for faithfulness in any area of Christian living, including giving. Spiritual blessing (Eph. 1:3) and the meeting of material needs (Phil. 4:19) are what God promises. Being prospered materially is no necessary sign of deep godliness of faithful tithing; and contrariwise, poverty is no indication of being out of God's will (cf. Paul's own case in Phil. 4:12)....

Proportionate giving is not starting with a tithe and then doing what more we can when we can. Proportionate giving is giving as God hath prospered. If someone felt after prayer that the right proportion for him should be 10 percent, I would suggest that he gives 9 or 11 percent just to keep out of the 10 percent rut. A person who is giving 9 or 11 percent will find himself much more sensitive to the Lord's changing his proportion than if he were giving 10 percent.

Every believer owes 100 percent of what he is and what he has to God. The question, then, is not only how much I give, but also how much I spend on myself. Proportionate giving alone can furnish the right answer to this matter and for every stage of life. We give because He gave, not because He commanded;

we give because we want to, not because we have to; we give because we love Him, and we show that love most concretely in this way. If in turn God blesses us materially, we praise Him; if not, we still praise Him. This is grace giving, and this is the proof of our love for God.[67]

[67] Charles Caldwell Ryrie, *Balancing the Christian Life* (Chicago, IL: Moody Press, 1969), 87-89.

APPENDIX B

Quote from Warren and David Wiersbe with Scriptural Support

The following resource has added supporting Scriptures to the ten statements about the ministry found in Warren and David Wiersbe, *Making Sense of the Ministry.*[68]

1. The foundation of ministry is character.

> Acts 6:3 "Therefore, brethren, select from among you seven men of good reputation, full of the Spirit and of wisdom, whom we may put in charge of this task."
>
> Philippians 2:14–16 "Do all things without grumbling or disputing; so that you will prove yourselves to be blameless and innocent, children of God above reproach in the midst of a crooked and perverse generation, among whom you appear as lights in the world, holding fast the word of life, so that

---

[68] Warren and David Wiersbe, *Making Sense of the Ministry* (Grand Rapids: Baker Books, 1983), 31-46, as cited in Charles R. Swindoll, *Rise and Shine: A Wake-up Call* (Portland, OR: Multinomah, 1989), 41.

in the day of Christ I will have reason to glory because I did not run in vain nor toil in vain."

1 Thessalonians 5:21–23 "But examine everything carefully; hold fast to that which is good; abstain from every form of evil. Now may the God of peace Himself sanctify you entirely; and may your spirit and soul and body be preserved complete, without blame at the coming of our Lord Jesus Christ."

2 Timothy 2:24–25 "The Lord's bond-servant must not be quarrelsome, but be kind to all, able to teach, patient when wronged, with gentleness correcting those who are in opposition, if perhaps God may grant them repentance leading to the knowledge of the truth."

2. The nature of ministry is service.

Matthew 20:26–28 "It is not this way among you, but whoever wishes to become great among you shall be your servant, and whoever wishes to be first among you shall be your slave; just as the Son of Man did not come to be served, but to serve, and to give His life a ransom for many."

Romans 12:10–14 "Be devoted to one another in brotherly love; give preference to one another in honor; not lagging behind in diligence, fervent in spirit, serving the Lord; rejoicing in hope, persevering in tribulation, devoted to prayer, contributing to the needs of the saints, practicing hospitality."

1 Peter 2:5, 9 "you also, as living stones, are being built up as a spiritual house for a holy priesthood,

to offer up spiritual sacrifices acceptable to God through Jesus Christ. But you are a chosen race, a royal priesthood, a holy nation, a people for God's own possession, so that you may proclaim the excellencies of Him who has called you out of darkness into His marvelous light."

1 Peter 4:10–11 "As each one has received a special gift, employ it in serving one another as good stewards of the manifold grace of God. Whoever speaks, is to do so as one who is speaking the utterances of God; whoever serves is to do so as one who is serving by the strength which God supplies; so that in all things God may be glorified through Jesus Christ, to whom belongs the glory and dominion forever and ever. Amen."

3. The motive for ministry is love.

    John 15:12 "This is My commandment, that you love one another, just as I have loved you."

    Galatians 5:13 "For you were called to freedom, brethren; only do not turn your freedom into an opportunity for the flesh, but through love serve one another."

    1 Thessalonians 1:2–3 "We give thanks to God always for all of you, making mention of you in our prayers; constantly bearing in mind your work of faith and labor of love and steadfastness of hope in our Lord Jesus Christ in the presence of our God and Father."

4. The measure of ministry is sacrifice.

John 15:13 "Greater love has no one than this, that one lay down his life for his friends."

Romans 12:1 "Therefore I urge you, brethren, by the mercies of God, to present your bodies a living and holy sacrifice, acceptable to God, which is your spiritual service of worship."

Hebrews 13:15-16 "Through Him then, let us continually offer up a sacrifice of praise to God, that is, the fruit of lips that give thanks to His name. And do not neglect doing good and sharing, for with such sacrifices God is pleased."

5. The authority of ministry is submission.

John 15:14 "You are My friends if you do what I command you."

Romans 13:1-5 "Every person is to be in subjection to the governing authorities. For there is no authority except from God, and those which exist are established by God. Therefore whoever resists authority has opposed the ordinance of God; and they who have opposed will receive condemnation upon themselves. For rulers are not a cause of fear for good behavior, but for evil. Do you want to have no fear of authority? Do what is good and you will have praise from the same; for it is a minister of God to you for good. But if you do what is evil, be afraid; for it does not bear the sword for nothing; for it is a minister of God, an avenger who brings wrath on the one who practices evil. Therefore it is necessary to be in subjection, not only because of wrath, but also for conscience' sake."

Titus 3:1–2 "Remind them to be subject to rulers, to authorities, to be obedient, to be ready for every good deed, to malign no one, to be peaceable, gentle, showing every consideration for all men."

James 4:7a "Submit therefore to God."

1 Peter 2:13, 18, 23 "Submit yourselves for the Lord's sake to every human institution, whether to a king as the one in authority,... Servants, be submissive to your masters with all respect, not only to those who are good and gentle, but also to those who are unreasonable...and while being reviled, He did not revile in return; while suffering, He uttered no threats, but kept entrusting Himself to Him who judges righteously."

1 Peter 5:5–7 "You younger men, likewise, be subject to your elders; and all of you, clothe yourselves with humility toward one another, for God is opposed to the proud, but gives grace to the humble. Therefore humble yourselves under the mighty hand of God, that He may exalt you at the proper time, casting all your anxiety on Him, because He cares for you."

6. The purpose of ministry is the glory of God.

Romans 11:33–36 "Oh, the depth of the riches both of the wisdom and knowledge of God! How unsearchable are His judgments and unfathomable His ways! For who has known the mind of the Lord, or who became His counselor? Or who has first given to Him that it might be paid back to him again? For from Him and through Him and to Him are all things. To Him be the glory forever. Amen."

1 Corinthians 6:20 "For you have been bought with a price: therefore glorify God in your body."

1 Corinthians 10:31 "Whether, then, you eat or drink or whatever you do, do all to the glory of God."

Colossians 3:23–24 "Whatever you do, do your work heartily, as for the Lord rather than for men, knowing that from the Lord you will receive the reward of the inheritance. It is the Lord Christ whom you serve."

7. The tools of ministry are the Word of God and prayer.

Ephesians 6:17b–18 "And take...the sword of the Spirit, which is the word of God. With all prayer and petition pray at all times in the Spirit, and with this in view, be on the alert with all perseverance and petition for all the saints."

James 1:22–25 "But prove yourselves doers of the word, and not merely hearers who delude themselves. For if anyone is a hearer of the word and not a doer, he is like a man who looks at his natural face in a mirror; for once he has looked at himself and gone away, he has immediately forgotten what kind of person he was. But one who looks intently at the perfect law, the law of liberty, and abides by it, not having become a forgetful hearer but an effectual doer, this man will be blessed in what he does."

1 Timothy 2:1–2, 8 "First of all, then, I urge that entreaties and prayers, petitions and thanksgivings, be made on behalf of all men, for kings and all who are in authority, so that we may lead a tranquil and quiet life in all godliness and dignity.... Therefore I want the men in every place to pray, lifting up holy hands, without wrath and dissension."

2 Timothy 3:16–17 "All Scripture is inspired by God and profitable for teaching, for reproof, for correction, for training in righteousness; so that the man of God may be adequate, equipped for every good work."

8. The privilege of ministry is growth.

John 15:8, 15–17 "My Father is glorified by this, that you bear much fruit, and so prove to be My disciples.... No longer do I call you slaves, for the slave does not know what his master is doing; but I have called you friends, for all things that I have heard from My Father I have made known to you. You did not choose Me but I chose you, and appointed you that you would go and bear fruit, and that your fruit would remain, so that whatever you ask of the Father in My name He may give to you. This I command you, that you love one another."

Ephesians 4:15–16 "but speaking the truth in love, we are to grow up in all aspects into Him who is the head, even Christ, from whom the whole body, being fitted and held together by what every joint supplies, according to the proper working of each individual part, causes the growth of the body for the building up of itself in love."

Colossians 3:12–17 "So, as those who have been chosen of God, holy and beloved, put on a heart of compassion, kindness, humility, gentleness and patience; bearing with one another, and forgiving each other, whoever has a complaint against anyone; just as the Lord forgave you, so also should you. Beyond all these things put on love, which is the perfect bond of unity. Let the peace of Christ rule in your hearts, to which indeed you were called in one body; and be thankful. Let the word of Christ richly dwell within you, with all wisdom teaching and admonishing one another with psalms and hymns and spiritual songs, singing with thankfulness in your hearts to God. Whatever you do in word or deed, do all in the name of the Lord Jesus, giving thanks through Him to God the Father."

9. The power of ministry is the Holy Spirit.

Acts 1:8 "but you will receive power when the Holy Spirit has come upon you; and you shall be My witnesses both in Jerusalem, and in all Judea and Samaria, and even to the remotest part of the earth."

Romans 7:6 "But now we have been released from the Law, having died to that by which we were bound, so that we serve in newness of the Spirit and not in oldness of the letter."

Ephesians 3:16 "that He would grant you, according to the riches of His glory, to be strengthened with power through His Spirit in the inner man."

10. The model for ministry is Jesus Christ.

Philippians 2:5–11 "Have this attitude in yourselves which was also in Christ Jesus, who, although He existed in the form of God, did not regard equality with God a thing to be grasped, but emptied Himself, taking the form of a bond-servant, and being made in the likeness of men. Being found in appearance as a man, He humbled Himself by becoming obedient to the point of death, even death on a cross. For this reason also, God highly exalted Him, and bestowed on Him the name which is above every name, so that at the name of Jesus EVERY KNEE WILL BOW, of those who are in heaven and on earth and under the earth, and that every tongue will confess that Jesus Christ is Lord, to the glory of God the Father."

1 Peter 2:19–23 "For this finds favor, if for the sake of conscience toward God a person bears up under sorrows when suffering unjustly. For what credit is there if, when you sin and are harshly treated, you endure it with patience? But if when you do what is right and suffer for it you patiently endure it, this finds favor with God. For you have been called for this purpose, since Christ also suffered for you, leaving you an example for you to follow in His steps, who committed no sin, nor was any deceit found in His mouth; and while being reviled, He did not revile in return; while suffering, He uttered no threats, but kept entrusting Himself to Him who judges righteously."

APPENDIX C

Suggested Reading

Ted W. Engstrom and R. Alec Mackenzie, *Managing Your Time* (Grand Rapids, MI: Zondervan, 1967).

Gene A. Getz, *A Biblical Theology Of Material Possessions* (Chicago, IL: Moody Publishers, 1990).

Gene A. Getz, *Real Prosperity: Biblical Principles Of Material Possessions* (Chicago, IL: Moody Publishers, 1990).

Woodrow Kroll, *Taking Back the Good Book* (Wheaton, IL: Good News Publishers, 2007).

Steven J. Larson, *Famine in the Land: A Passionate Call for Expository Preaching* (Chicago, IL: Moody Publishers, 2003).

Aubrey Malphurs & Steve Stroope, *Money Matters In Church* (Grand Rapids, MI: Baker Books, 2007).

Alfred Martin, *Not My Own* (Chicago, IL: Moody Press, 1968). Also reprint edition - Alfred Martin, *Biblical Stewardship* (Dubuque, IA: ECS Ministries, revised 2005, reprinted 2010, 2014).

Kirk Nowery, *The Stewardship of Life* (Camarillo, CA: Spire Resources, Inc., Publishers, 2004).

Stephen F. Olford, *The Grace Of Giving-A Biblical Study Of Christian Stewardship* Revised Edition (Grand Rapids, MI: Kregel Publications, 1972, 2000).

Charles C. Ryrie, *Balancing the Christian Life* (Chicago, IL: Moody Press, 1969).

Charles C. Ryrie, *Dispensationalism*, Revised and Expanded (Chicago, IL: Moody Press, 1995, 2007).

Charlie W. Shedd, *Time for All Things* (Nashville, TN: Abingdon Press, 1962).

John Stott, *The Grace of Giving-Ten Principles of Giving* (Peabody, MA: Hendrickson Publishers, 2004).

Printed in the United States
By Bookmasters